First World War
and Army of Occupation
War Diary
France, Belgium and Germany

28 DIVISION
Divisional Troops
Royal Army Medical Corps
86 Field Ambulance
14 January 1915 - 30 October 1915

WO95/2272/7

The Naval & Military Press Ltd
www.nmarchive.com
Published in association with The National Archives

Published by

The Naval & Military Press Ltd

Unit 10 Ridgewood Industrial Park,

Uckfield, East Sussex,

TN22 5QE England

Tel: +44 (0) 1825 749494

www.naval-military-press.com

www.nmarchive.com

This diary has been reprinted in facsimile from the original. Any imperfections are inevitably reproduced and the quality may fall short of modern type and cartographic standards.

© **Crown Copyright**
Images reproduced by permission of The National Archives, London, England, 2015.

Contents

Document type	Place/Title	Date From	Date To
Heading	WO95/2272/7		
Heading	28th Division Medical 86th Fld Ambulance Jan-Oct 1915		
Heading	86th Field Ambulance (Northum Trian) Vol I		
War Diary	Winchester	14/01/1915	18/01/1915
War Diary	Southampton	18/01/1915	18/01/1915
War Diary	Havre	19/01/1915	21/01/1915
War Diary	Hazebrouck	22/01/1915	22/01/1915
War Diary	Caestre	22/01/1915	31/01/1915
Diagram etc	Sketch Shewing Billets Occupied In Caestre		
War Diary	Caestre	01/02/1915	02/02/1915
War Diary	Ouderdom	02/02/1915	09/03/1915
Diagram etc	Map Show Opositions Of Battalions In 85th Brigade		
Heading	121/4808 March 1915 86th (2nd Northum Trian) Field Ambulance Vol II		
War Diary	Ouderdom	13/03/1915	31/03/1915
Miscellaneous	Transport Diary	09/03/1915	09/03/1915
Miscellaneous	Transport Diary		
Heading	121/5320 April 1915 86th Field Ambulance Vol III		
War Diary	Ouderdom	01/04/1915	05/04/1915
War Diary	Hoofgraaf	06/04/1915	08/04/1915
War Diary	Ypres	09/04/1915	21/04/1915
War Diary	Poperinghe	22/04/1915	30/04/1915
Heading	28th Division 86th (2nd Northum Trian) Field Ambulance Vol IV May 1915		
War Diary	Farm Near To Poperinghe	01/05/1915	14/05/1915
War Diary	Farm Near To Watou	15/05/1915	19/05/1915
War Diary	Farm Near To Herzeele	20/05/1915	22/05/1915
War Diary	Farm Near To Poperinghe	22/05/1915	30/05/1915
War Diary	Farm Near To Watou	31/05/1915	31/05/1915
Heading	121/5875 28th Division 86th Field Ambulance Vol V June 1915		
War Diary	Farm Near To Watou	01/06/1915	20/06/1915
War Diary	Farm Near To Boeschepe	21/06/1915	30/06/1915
Heading	28th Division 121/6341 86th Field Ambulance July 1915 Vol VI		
War Diary	Farm Near Boescheppe	01/07/1915	16/07/1915
War Diary	La Clytte	16/07/1915	22/07/1915
War Diary	Westoutre	22/07/1915	24/07/1915
War Diary	Locre	24/07/1915	31/07/1915
Heading	28th Division 86th Field Ambulance Vol VII Aug. Sept & Oct 15		
War Diary	Locre	01/08/1915	20/09/1915
War Diary	Bethune	01/10/1915	20/10/1915
War Diary	Locre	21/10/1915	25/10/1915
War Diary	Bethune	27/10/1915	27/10/1915
War Diary	Sailly Le Bourse	28/10/1915	29/10/1915
War Diary	Bethune	29/10/1915	30/10/1915

John 2222/5045 (7)

John 2222/5045

28TH DIVISION
MEDICAL

86TH FLD AMBULANCE
JAN-OCT 1915

121/46/11
Jan 1915
Dec 1915

86th Field Ambulance (Northumbrian)

Vol I.

Army Form C. 2118

2nd NORTHUMBRIAN FIELD AMBULANCE,
ROYAL ARMY MEDICAL CORPS. (T.F.)

WAR DIARY
or
INTELLIGENCE SUMMARY.
(Erase heading not required.)

Instructions regarding War Diaries and Intelligence Summaries are contained in F.S. Regs., Part II. and the Staff Manual respectively. Title pages will be prepared in manuscript.

Hour, Date, Place	Summary of Events and Information	Remarks and references to Appendices
11.30 p.m 16.1.15 WINCHESTER	Received Orders to provide a Billeting Party to report at SOUTHAMPTON	JHC
17-1-15 "	The 2nd Northumbrian Field Ambulance being fully up to strength in personnel, and having been completely re-equipped with clothing, vehicles, and extra horses, but not with Motor Ambulances received instructions to proceed to SOUTHAMPTON	JHC
9.35 a.m 18.1.15	Paraded and proceeded as per instructions above. Officers Lieut Col. D.A. CAMERON. Major D.V. HAIG. Major D.L. FISHER. Capt G.R. ELLIS. Lieut WILSON. Lieut H WARDLE. Lieut E.P. SCOTT. Lieut and Qr master E LYALL. Lieut & Transport Officer. Lieut A FERENS, and Rev. F.S. SCOTT Chaplain. with 231. N.C. Os & men. The Transport consisted of 15 riding horses, 47 heavy draught, 17 pair. wheeled vehicles and 4 two wheel vehicles. The weather was sunny & frosty; roads dry; Unit marched well and no men fell out.	

Forms/C. 2118/10   (9 29 6) W 4141—403 100,000 9/14 H W V

2ND NORTHUMBRIAN FIELD AMBULANCE
ROYAL ARMY MEDICAL CORPS.
Army Form C. 2118.

WAR DIARY
or
INTELLIGENCE SUMMARY.
(Erase heading not required.)

Instructions regarding War Diaries and Intelligence Summaries are contained in F.S. Regs., Part II. and the Staff Manual respectively. Title pages will be prepared in manuscript.

Hour, Date, Place	Summary of Events and Information	Remarks and references to Appendices
9.40pm 18-1-15 SOUTHAMPTON	Arrived No 2. Dock Gate and embarked on H.M.T.S. BELLEROPHON.	D.H.C
12.0 noon. 19-1-15 HAVRE	Arrived and disembarked	D.H.C
9.0 pm	Arrived at rest camp SAINT ADRESSE.	
2.30 pm 20-1-15 do	Goat skin coats issued to the men. Continuous rain	
11.0 pm do	Paraded and proceeded to GARE DU MARCHANDISE. (Point 3). HAVRE	
12.0 midnight to 5.30 am 21-1-15 do	Loaded equipment and entrained for HAZEBROUCK	D.H.C
4.45 am 22-1-15 HAZEBROUCK	Arrived Equipment unloaded and men handed — proceeded to CAESTRE. On the road met Lt. A.D.M.S. (Col ALLEN) who enquired about our journey	
12.0 noon 22-1-15 CAESTRE	Arrival at CAESTRE	D.H.C

Army Form C. 2118.

2nd NORTHUMBRIAN FIELD AMBULANCE,
ROYAL ARMY MEDICAL CORPS. (T.F.)

WAR DIARY
or
INTELLIGENCE SUMMARY.
(Erase heading not required.)

Instructions regarding War Diaries and Intelligence Summaries are contained in F. S. Regs., Part II. and the Staff Manual respectively. Title pages will be prepared in manuscript.

Hour, Date, Place		Summary of Events and Information	Remarks and references to Appendices
22-1-15	CAESTRE	Billeted in 2 farms and Hospice Communal. Hospital opened in "A" Section tents & wagons in the latter place under Capt. ELLIS and Lieut LAWRENCE. Accommodation for 30 patients. Attended 2 conferences at Div. H. Qrs. on prevention of frost bite, use of whale oil and anti frost bite grease, arrival of 5 motor ambulances - part transport establishment Motor Workshop Unit Divisional attached under Lieut HEWITT A.S.C. D.D.M.S. Lt Col FERGUSON C.M.G relieved Col ALLEN. (ie)	JAG
28.1.15	- do -	Inspection of troops of XXVII Division by the C-in-C Sir J. FRENCH, accompanied by H.R.H. Prince of Wales	JAG
29.1.15	- do -	Lieut E. P. SCOTT took up duties as Sanitary Officer to Brigade - 83rd Brigade Field Day.	JAG
31-1-15	do.	Lieut E. P. SCOTT transferred to Co. C. Hosp. (Influenza)	JAG

2ND NORTHUMBRIAN FIELD AMBULANCE
ROYAL ARMY MEDICAL CORPS.

Map I.

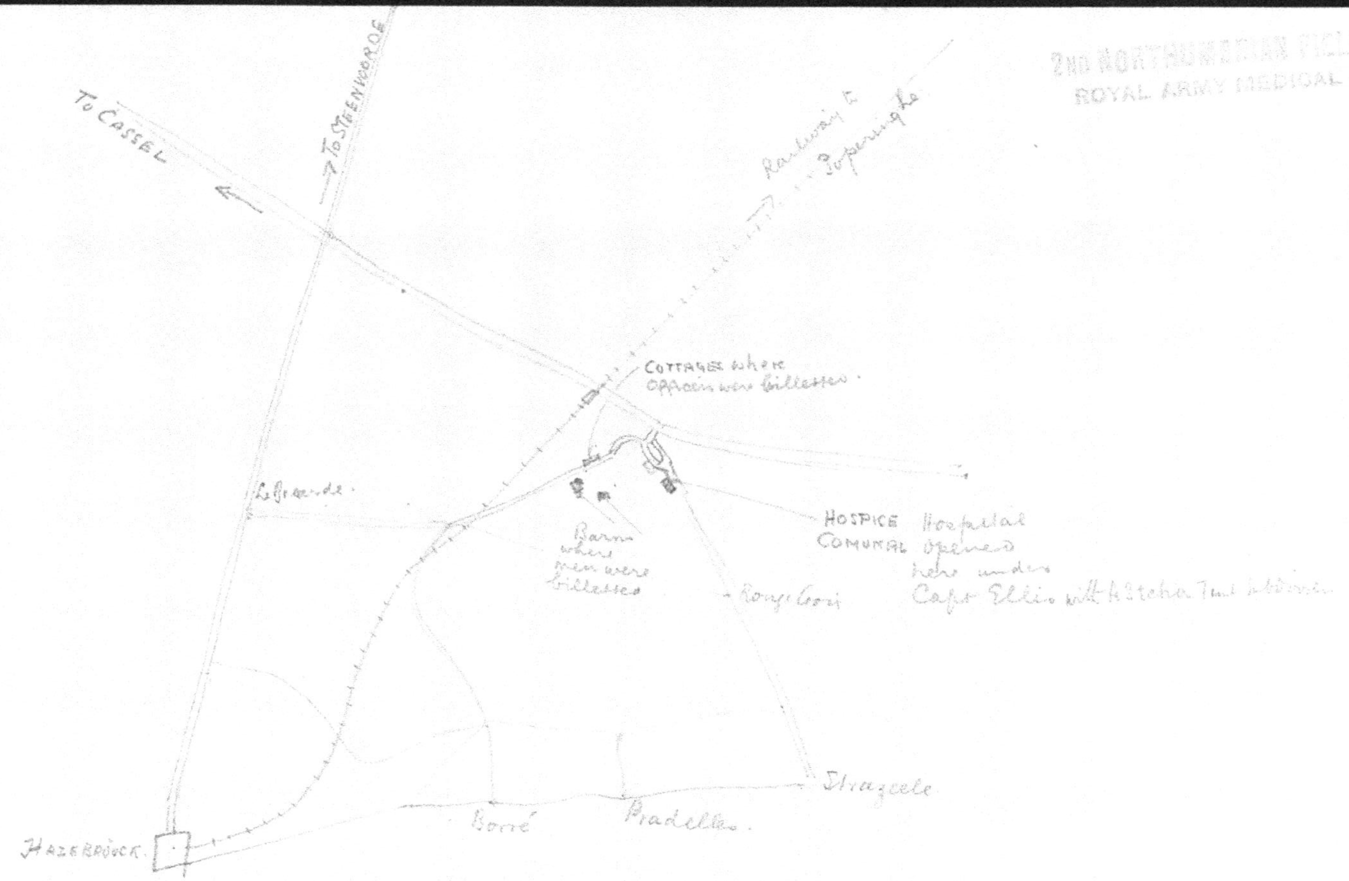

SKETCH
SHEWING BILLETS
OCCUPIED IN
CAESTRE.

To Cassel
To Steenwoorde
Hazebrouck
La Grande
Borre
Pradelles
Strazeele
Cottages where Officers were billetted
Barn where men were billetted
Hospice Communal Opened for wounded
Royalons
Capt. Ellis with kitchen and latrines

Army Form C. 2118.

WAR DIARY
or
INTELLIGENCE SUMMARY.
(Erase heading not required.)

2ND NORTHUMBRIAN FIELD AMBULANCE,
ROYAL ARMY MEDICAL CORPS. (T.F.)

Instructions regarding War Diaries and Intelligence Summaries are contained in F.S. Regs., Part II. and the Staff Manual respectively. Title pages will be prepared in manuscript.

Hour, Date, Place		Summary of Events and Information	Remarks and references to Appendices
	CHESTRE	The billets occupied were barns which were over-run with rats and mice. The water was obtained from pumps. All water was boiled before using. Latrine accommodation was specially dug.	
1-2-15		The 15th January Section under Lieut DRAYCOTT was attached for duty. Lieut A.C.C. LAWRENCE transferred to Cas Cl Hosp – Influenza. Major WINGATE R.A.M.C attached (10 days) to assist O.C. with advice. Surg Gen PORTER D.M.S. at BÔRRE	JKG
2-2-15		Hospital Closed; Number of patients treated (200) mostly influenza, some pneumonia, and one self inflicted wound. (31-1-15) Paraded and marched to OUDERDOM with 85th Brigade under Brigadier General CHAPMAN	JKG
9.0 am 2-2-15			JKG
4.0 pm	OUDERDOM.	Arrived. Billeted in 3 barns. Hospital in the	JKG

Army Form C. 2118.

WAR DIARY
or
INTELLIGENCE SUMMARY.
(Erase heading not required.)

2nd NORTHUMBRIAN FIELD AMBULANCE,
ROYAL ARMY MEDICAL CORPS. (T.F.)

Instructions regarding War Diaries and Intelligence Summaries are contained in F.S. Regs., Part II. and the Staff Manual respectively. Title pages will be prepared in manuscript.

Hour, Date, Place	Summary of Events and Information	Remarks and references to Appendices
	HERBERG DEN OUDERDOM – accommodation 30 and 60 in an adjacent barn. Hospital in charge of Major HAIG. The premises were found to be in a very insanitary state – previously used by the French as a General Hospital – thoroughly cleaned and disinfected and water supply examined – found to be bad. Men billeted in barns in which they lie on straw infested with rats, mice, and lice. Billets are quite warm but offensive owing to the manure deposits in the farm yards. Water supply from pumps. All water to be boiled or disinfected by chloride of lime in water carts. At Ellen ? wires by CAPT ELLIS. Popering ? Rohin by ? WILSON.	

Forms/C. 2118/10

Army Form C. 2118.

WAR DIARY
or
INTELLIGENCE SUMMARY.
(Erase heading not required.)

2ND NORTHUMBRIAN FIELD AMBULANCE,
ROYAL ARMY MEDICAL CORPS. (T.F.)

Instructions regarding War Diaries and Intelligence Summaries are contained in F.S. Regs., Part II. and the Staff Manual respectively. Title pages will be prepared in manuscript.

Hour, Date, Place	Summary of Events and Information	Remarks and references to Appendices
8.0 pm 4.2.15 OUDERDOM	Men paraded and proceeded to YPRES under Major HAIG, Capt ELLIS, and Lieut WARDLE, the bearer division having been ordered to assist the 85th (3rd [order]) 1st Field Ambulance in collecting wounded.	JK
1.0 am 5-2-15 "	Troops returned – as they were not required.	
6-2-15 "	Lieut WARDLE transferred to hosp. des Ypres (Influenza)	
7-2-15 "	Major HAIG transferred to Cas. de Hop. (Influenza)	
7-2-15 "	Major FISHER, O/I/c of Hospital.	
7-2-15 "	No. of patients admitted during week 71.	JK
8.2.15	Under verbal instructions from the A.D.M.S. a Convalescent Rest Station is to be opened in STEENVOORDE. Billets were obtained in the schools at the Mairie and in the town schools. These billets were in a very insanitary condition and the latrine accommodation totally inadequate. The total	

Army Form C. 2118.

WAR DIARY
or
INTELLIGENCE SUMMARY.
(*Erase heading not required.*)

2nd NORTHUMBRIAN FIELD AMBULANCE
ROYAL ARMY MEDICAL CORPS. (T.F.)

Instructions regarding War Diaries and Intelligence Summaries are contained in F.S. Regs., Part II. and the Staff Manual respectively. Title pages will be prepared in manuscript.

Hour, Date, Place	Summary of Events and Information	Remarks and references to Appendices

accomodation is to be for 600 patients. The billets have been thoroughly cleaned and are now in good condition. The object of this Convalescent Rest Station is for resting the men after treatment in the Field Ambulances and thereby preventing wastage to Units by men being sent down to the Base and lost sight of in consequence. The establishment of a Convalescent Rest Station by a Field Ambulance is an innovation and not provided for in the establishment for Field Ambulances; the result being that an Imprest a/c was necessary to provide for its equipment-

Army Form C. 2118.

WAR DIARY
or
INTELLIGENCE SUMMARY.
(Erase heading not required.)

2nd NORTHUMBRIAN FIELD AMBULANCE,
ROYAL ARMY MEDICAL CORPS, (T.F.)

Instructions regarding War Diaries and Intelligence Summaries are contained in F.S. Regs., Part II. and the Staff Manual respectively. Title pages will be prepared in manuscript.

Hour, Date, Place	Summary of Events and Information	Remarks and references to Appendices
	to provide beds, hot baths, stretchers, blankets, and cooking utensils & change of clothing are provided when necessary. The Officer i/c is Major WINGATE, who is assisted by Capt ELLIS. The Field Ambulance is now carrying out the three zones of the Medical Organization - viz:- Collecting Wounded, Field Hospital, and Convalescent Rest Station.	
8.0 a.m. 11-2-15. ODDERDOM	"B" Section paraded and marched to STEENVOORDE accompanied by "C" Section Transport Section and 1 Motor Ambulance	
13.2.15	Major HAIG and Lieut WARDLE returned from hospital to duty.	
4 p.m. 15-2-15	Bearer division paraded and proceeded to YPRES to collect wounded	

Army Form C. 2118.

2nd NORTHUMBRIAN FIELD AMBULANCE,
ROYAL ARMY MEDICAL CORPS, (T.F.)

WAR DIARY
or
INTELLIGENCE SUMMARY.
(Erase heading not required.)

Instructions regarding War Diaries and Intelligence Summaries are contained in F. S. Regs., Part II. and the Staff Manual respectively. Title pages will be prepared in manuscript.

Hour, Date, Place	Summary of Events and Information	Remarks and references to Appendices
	The patients admitted during last week — most of whom suffered from so called frost-bite. The milder cases complain of insensibility in the toes and tingling of the feet without swelling or discolouration. The worst cases showed great swelling of the feet and legs with dark blue discolouration of the toes, which when destroyed not only enormously but had lost all sensation and power of movement. Blebs appeared and yellow serum oozing in drops from a fun head to a walnut, appeared on the dorsum of the feet and toes. After washing the feet in Hydrogen Peroxide and opening	

WAR DIARY
or
INTELLIGENCE SUMMARY.

(Erase heading not required.)

Army Form C. 2118.

2ND NORTHUMBRIAN FIELD AMBULANCE,
ROYAL ARMY MEDICAL CORPS, (T.F.)

Hour, Date, Place	Summary of Events and Information	Remarks and references to Appendices
	the blisters and gentle massage, they were dusted with boric powder, dressed with cotton wool and the feet elevated. In some cases the feet were so swollen that the boots had to be cut off. All these patients complained of great pain in walking and the worst cases were unable to stand. Many of our patients had recently arrived from India and were in a low state of health. Their clothing was good and warm and their food sound, but owing to the depth of water and mud, together with decaying organic matter in the trenches, their feet were never always wet and cold, and exposed to septic organisms. Few officers were affected	

Army Form C. 2118.

WAR DIARY
or
INTELLIGENCE SUMMARY.
(Erase heading not required.)

2ND NORTHUMBRIAN FIELD AMBULANCE
ROYAL ARMY MEDICAL CORPS. (T.F.)

Hour, Date, Place	Summary of Events and Information	Remarks and references to Appendices
5.15 am. 15-2-15 OUDEROOM	Received orders for Bearers to proceed to YPRES	
6.10 am	Bearer subdivision paraded and marched to YPRES under command of Major FISHER.	
10.p.m.	Bent division returned	
6 p.m. 17-2-15 "	Bearers paraded and proceeded to YPRES to collect wounded. Lieut WILSON attached to Buffs as R.M.O. Lieut WARDLE temporarily attached to E Yorks to replace Lieut CAMPBELL killed	M.O. M.O.
5 a.m 18-2-15 "	Bearers returned	
9.30 am 19-2-15. "	"C" Section bent sub division paraded and dispatched to STEENVOORDE Convalescent Rest Station. Lieut T D INCH joined Unit "B" Section Bearers arrived from STEENVOORDE, Lieut WARDLE returned to Unit	M.O.
4 p.m 21.2.15 "	No of patients admitted during week 283. Lieut D.R.G. ROBERTS (temp Lieut RAMC) attached for duty	

Army Form C. 2118.

2ND NORTHUMBRIAN FIELD AMBULANCE,
ROYAL ARMY MEDICAL CORPS. (T.F.)

WAR DIARY
or
INTELLIGENCE SUMMARY.
(Erase heading not required.)

Instructions regarding War Diaries and Intelligence Summaries are contained in F.S. Regs., Part II. and the Staff Manual respectively. Title pages will be prepared in manuscript.

Hour, Date, Place	Summary of Events and Information	Remarks and references to Appendices
21.2.15 OUDEROOM	"A" Section Medical Store cart and G.S. wagon sent to STEENVOORDE.	JMG
22.2.15	Major FISHER accompanied by Lieut EPSCOTT, dropped to STEENVOORDE to understudy Major WINGATE	JMG
5.30pm 24.2.15	Bearer division paraded and went to YPRES. PT. STARK shot through ankle	JMG
6.0 am 25.2.15	Bearers returned. Officers have been detailed to visit battalions and detail which have no regimental M.O. attached. The sick are collected by horsed ambulances. Once daily a Motor lorry calls to evacuate the sick and wounded to the Clear. Hosp. Hspl.	
27.2.15	Lieut A.C.C. LAWRENCE Transferred to Coo. Clg. Hspl (Sicilia)	JMG

Army Form C. 2118

WAR DIARY
or
INTELLIGENCE SUMMARY.
(Erase heading not required.)

2/1 NORTHUMBRIAN FIELD AMBULANCE
ROYAL ARMY MEDICAL CORPS. (T.F.)

Instructions regarding War Diaries and Intelligence Summaries are contained in F.S. Regs., Part II. and the Staff Manual respectively. Title pages will be prepared in manuscript.

Hour, Date, Place		Summary of Events and Information	Remarks and references to Appendices
	28-2-15 OUDEROOM	No: of patients admitted during week - 307.	
	3-3-15 "	Chaplain Rev F.E. SCOTT relieves My Chaplain Rev. E.A. FITCH. (Cof E)	
6 p.m.	4-3-15 "	Bearer division paraded and went to YPRES. Bearer division returned.	
5.30 a.m.	5-3-15 "	The A.D.M.S. accompanied by the O.C. and Divisional Sanitary Officer visited the Brigade Camp of Ants, recently erected, to choose a new water supply. The previous temporary arrangement provided a supply both poor in quality and quantity, and was obtained from several pumps in the farm yards where the troops have been billeted. The A.D.M.S. in conjunction with the O.C., the Camp Commandant (Capt Agg) and Capt Copland (Army Corps Bacteriologist) examined the new water supply and a

(9 29 6) W 4141—463 100,000 9/14 H W V Forms/C. 2118/10

WAR DIARY
or
INTELLIGENCE SUMMARY.
(Erase heading not required.)

Hour, Date, Place	Summary of Events and Information	Remarks and references to Appendices
	report by the last mentioned will be furnished as soon as possible. The Regimental MO's have been instructed to sterilize all water used, and all men's water bottles are to be filled each evening with freshly boiled water. Latrines have been dug in suitable places. The huts, which have been erected and inspected, have timber frames covered with coarse canvas sack cloth, which when not tarred lets through the rain water freely. Some of the huts have tarred canvas covering and boarded floors raised well above the ground and are quite dry. Fresh straw has been put down and the men state they are quite warm and comfortable. In those huts with unboarded	

2nd NORTHUMBRIAN FIELD AMBULANCE,
ROYAL ARMY MEDICAL CORPS. (T.F.)

Army Form C. 2118

WAR DIARY
or
INTELLIGENCE SUMMARY.
(Erase heading not required.)

Instructions regarding War Diaries and Intelligence Summaries are contained in F.S. Regs., Part II. and the Staff Manual respectively. Title pages will be prepared in manuscript.

Hour, Date, Place	Summary of Events and Information	Remarks and references to Appendices
March 10/15 OUDERDOM. 4-5pm 8+3-15	floors where the straw was placed direct on the ground, the floor is moist and sour smelling. These were cleaned and fresh straw put down. Number of cases admitted during week - 322.	JG
"	The A.D.M.S. visited the Field Ambulance. Received verbal instructions recalling	JG
9-3-15	Major WINGATE from the Convalescent Rest Station. Major FISHER took over duties as Officer i/c of Convalescent Rest Station relieving Major WINGATE.	J Gilson

(9 29 6) W 4141—463 100,000 9/14 H W V Forms/C. 2118/10

2ND NORTHUMBRIAN FIELD AMBULANCE,
ROYAL ARMY MEDICAL CORPS. (T.F.)

Sketch
Map
I

POPERINGHE

Vlamertinghe.

* 12th London.

Brigade *
Head Quarters

* Buffs.

Shrine
Inn
Middlesex

* E. Surrey.

* Royal Fusiliers

Windmill
Farm Hospital
Shrine
Sickshed

OUDERDOM
Field Ambulance
2 Northumbrian

Billets
Farm

Map shewing positions
of Battalions in 85th Brigade

121/4803

121/4805
March 1915

86th (2nd Northumbrian) Field Ambulance

Vol II

Army Form C. 2118.

WAR DIARY
or
INTELLIGENCE SUMMARY.
(Erase heading not required.)

2nd Report 13/3/15
to 31/3/15

Instructions regarding War Diaries and Intelligence Summaries are contained in F.S. Regs., Part II. and the Staff Manual respectively. Title pages will be prepared in manuscript.

Hour, Date, Place	Summary of Events and Information	Remarks and references to Appendices
13-3-15 OUDERDOM.	The O.C. visited the A.D.M.S. - discussed the evacuation of suspected cases of supposed Cerebro Spinal Meningitis and Epilepsy. O.C. visited the Battalions in the Brigade area to which we are attached and discussed the water supply and general sanitation. The M.O.s were instructed in their duties by the A.D.M.S. A.D.M.S. visited 9th (Northumbrian) Field Ambulance Hospital and patients above referred to. During afternoon O.C. visited Convalescent Rest Station and found all satisfactory. The O/c reported that Millicent, Duchess of Sutherland had paid a visit. Col. CHOPPIN visited on 13th inst. and made additional arrangements for the reception of 310 wounded. Good accommodation has been found for these cases in the Salle du Bois of the Mairie (54 lying down) and in two rooms behind the Curé (28 lying down)	

Forms/C. 2118/10

Army Form C. 2118.

WAR DIARY
or
INTELLIGENCE SUMMARY.
(Erase heading not required.)

Instructions regarding War Diaries and Intelligence
Summaries are contained in F. S. Regs., Part II.
and the Staff Manual respectively. Title pages
will be prepared in manuscript.

Hour, Date, Place	Summary of Events and Information	Remarks and references to Appendices
9.50 pm 14-3-15 DUDEROOM	Three rooms are additional to place formerly placed at our disposal. In the room at the Mairie all furniture has been removed and the room thoroughly cleaned. Palliasses have been prepared & filled with clean straw. The rooms in the convent have been cleaned and ready.	
6.0 am 15-3-15 "	The D.A.D.M.S. viewed and gave instructions for the horses subdivisions to parade and proceed to YPRES to assist 2nd London Fd Amb) to collect wounded Lieut ROBERTS temporarily attached to No pick regiment. Bearers returned.	
" "	Visit of General Smith Dorrien (accompanied by A.D.M.S.) & field Ambulance Hospital at OUDEROOM	
11. 3. 15	Funeral of Driver Guilday and Sapper Yeomanry Sapr of Hitchwick conducted & preparations to accompany from granaries. Arrangement made for a new late supply	

Forms/C. 2118/10
(9 29 6) W 4111—463 100,000 9/14 H W V

Army Form C. 2118.

WAR DIARY
or
INTELLIGENCE SUMMARY.

(Erase heading not required.)

Instructions regarding War Diaries and Intelligence Summaries are contained in F.S. Regs., Part II. and the Staff Manual respectively. Title pages will be prepared in manuscript.

Hour, Date, Place	Summary of Events and Information	Remarks and references to Appendices
17 March 1915 OUDEROM	Visited billets of Artillery and Surrey Yeomanry. Visit of Col: BURRELL with reference to reinforcements from Reserve Unit. Baths & c. as to disposal in OUDEROM. Fresh clothing issued to patients requiring same	
11.45am. 18 - 3 - 15	Arrival of Reinforcement from Reserve Unit 2 NCOs and 10 men.	
21 - 3 - 15	No. of Patient admitted during week - 189	
24. 3. 15	The following report was received To O/C (Northumbrian F. Ambulance. In compliance with your orders I beg to report that I went this day to a farm on the Ouderdom - St Hubert - Halle bast Road when the Horse Transport and one section of the above Ambulance are billeted.	

Army Form C. 2118/10

WAR DIARY
or
INTELLIGENCE SUMMARY.
(Erase heading not required.)

Army Form C. 2118.

Instructions regarding War Diaries and Intelligence Summaries are contained in F. S. Regs., Part II. and the Staff Manual respectively. Title pages will be prepared in manuscript.

Hour, Date, Place	Summary of Events and Information	Remarks and references to Appendices
STEENVOORDE 24th March 1915	The woman who owns the farm asked me to report to you that several of her fields were occupied by either your carts, horses, or else used for football. She has four fields and she would be grateful if you would use only one of these in preference the one now used as a football field and also to put in these the carts and horses. This would allow she grass or crops to grow on the others and permit her to feed her cattle as her winter stock is rapidly coming to an end. On the other hand, she wishes you to know that she was very pleased with the attitude and behaviour of the troops and had absolutely no other grievance. A.J. Legendre Interpreter Attached	

WAR DIARY or INTELLIGENCE SUMMARY.

(Erase heading not required.)

Army Form C. 2118.

Hour, Date, Place	Summary of Events and Information	Remarks and references to Appendices
25 3.15 OUDERDOM	Received instructions to evacuate STEENVOORDE Convalescent Rest Station, the building being required as billets for a Brigade. With the Colonel and A.D.M.S. I visited some schools 2 miles from POPERINGHE. Though suitable in other ways they are too small and occupied by other troops. In the afternoon the A.D.M.S., Major FISHER and Capt. ELLIS inspected the Monastery at MT DES CATS, but found that building already in occupation of Cavalry and the North Midland Field Ambulance.	
26 3.15 "	Lieut ROBERTS detailed for Duty to the 1st Lincoln Regt.	
27 3.15 "	The following confidential circular (No 9) was received by Lieut. Colonel D.A. Cameron, OC 86th Field Ambulance. (1) Although in the ordinary way sick leave	

WAR DIARY
or
INTELLIGENCE SUMMARY.
(Erase heading not required.)

Army Form C. 2118.

Instructions regarding War Diaries and Intelligence Summaries are contained in F.S. Regs., Part II. and the Staff Manual respectively. Title pages will be prepared in manuscript.

Hour, Date, Place	Summary of Events and Information	Remarks and references to Appendices
	will be recommended only to patients who have been admitted to Hospitals at the Base; it is understood that in certain cases it may be necessary to recommend leave on sick certificate to those who have not been sent to such Hospitals. In these cases notes of the case should be sent to the office for the convenience of the Assistant Director of Medical Services before the recommendation for leave is submitted. (2) The practice of recommending Non-Commissioned Officers and men as fit for duty on the known or communication only should be restricted as much as possible; the Assistant Director of Medical Services should be personally consulted by Regimental Medical Officers before such recommendations are forwarded to Regimental Authorities. Defective eyesight in subjects who show no signs of emaciation are not to be considered as a disability. (3) Medical Officers are reminded that the premature diagnosis of infectious or contagious diseases	

WAR DIARY
or
INTELLIGENCE SUMMARY.
(Erase heading not required.)

Army Form C. 2118.

Hour, Date, Place	Summary of Events and Information	Remarks and references to Appendices
28. 3. 15	is apt to cause unnecessary alarm and despondency among troops. (Sgd.) Nicholas Ferguson Colonel A.M.S. A.D.M.S. 28th Division Exp. Force.	
29. 3. 15	O.C. visited Convalescent Rest Station at HOOGRAAF. which was full today. O.C. visited 6. R.S.	
30. 3. 15	A.D.M.S. gave instructions for Major HAIG for the erection of a Refreshment Shelter to be erected at the 6. R.S. This is to be done by means of tarpaulins. The O.C. visited the new Huts and inspected a new canteen just erected. O.C. visited O.C. Sanitary Section and made arrangements for the sterilization of water at the new canteen.	
31. 3. 15	Refreshment Shelter erected at C.R.S. The A.D.M.S. visited the C.R.S. There are now erected at the C.R.S. 8 Canadian Marquees, 3 Operating tents and a number of Bell tents. 1 Canadian Marquee is in the yard to hold stores.	

Army Form C. 2118.

WAR DIARY
or
INTELLIGENCE SUMMARY.
(Erase heading not required.)

Hour, Date, Place	Summary of Events and Information	Remarks and references to Appendices
31-3-15.	A Division Convalescent Rest Station has been established at HOOFGRAAF. (R.A.M Corps Order No 96. 31-3-15.	

Mch. 9th 1915.   Transport Diary.

Horses at Steenvoorde. 16 H.D. 5 Riders.
   "   " Ouderdom. 29 H.D. 12 " .
   "   Shout.   2 H.D.
Corp: Thompson returned to duty from Rouen Hospital.
Horses shod. 1 H.D. 3 Riders.

Mch. 11th A.D.M.S. & A.D.V.S. called to see horses. Clean bill
of health. Pair of horses Poperinghe for Coal, also a
pair to Ypres for Mail. Sent a pair to Poperinghe in the
afternoon for Medical Stores.

Mch. 12th Pair of horses sent to "Vlamertinghe" for
         the Mail.

" 13th Sent Lieut. Rohan's horse to Hospital. Lame.

" 14th Had all the equipement unloaded, & repacked.
        Sent a pair of horses to Poperinghe for Coal.
        also to Vlamertinghe for the Mail.

         2 H.D. and 1 R. shod.

Transport Diary.

Mch. 15: Horses c Steenvoorde. 16 H.D.
                                5 R.
        Do   c Ouderdom.   29 H.D.
                                11 R.
        Do Short. 2 H.D. 1 R.
        Had all the horses harnessed up, & men standing by.
Mch. 16: Transport Men Marched for baths.
" 19": Rec'd 2 H.D. horses. also 2 R. horses.
" 20": Pickets found a stray horse. Taken into our lines.

Transport Complete as regards horses & vehicles.
One Bat. Man short. viz. Walton.

H.D. 47
R. 18
    65 total.

121/5320

S 121/5320
April 1915.

86th Field Ambulance

Vol III

Army Form C. 2118.

WAR DIARY
or
INTELLIGENCE SUMMARY.
(Erase heading not required.)

Instructions regarding War Diaries and Intelligence Summaries are contained in F.S. Regs., Part II. and the Staff Manual respectively. Title pages will be prepared in manuscript.

Hour, Date, Place	Summary of Events and Information	Remarks and references to Appendices
14 April/15. Bustraat.	Visited Hut Camp awaith A.D.M.S. with reference to change of Battalions.	
2nd "	Sent ROBERTS rejoined unit after duty (temporary) with Lincoln Regt. Visited Hut Camp.	
3rd "	Full parade of unit at 9.30 am.	
7.30 am, 10.30 am	Hut inspection of unit. Inspection of waterworks. Visited Brigade Hors Camp under inspection from A.D.M.S. to investigate case of sudden death — Pte BURRELL — Norfolk Regt. — not due to his Lewis gun Apoplexy after exertion). Case of Zeppelin fever mentioned to H.Q./xxx/ from 6th Liverpool Irish.	M. Curry D.A. G.B. Mabbutt 86' Fd Amb 2nd Lieut Major Eva 2nd Lieut H
4th "	Visited Convalescent Rest Station. Major HAIG, on billeting officer, took over three farms near HOOFGRAAF, situated on	

Forms/C. 218/10

WAR DIARY
or
INTELLIGENCE SUMMARY.
(Erase heading not required.)

Army Form C. 2118.

Instructions regarding War Diaries and Intelligence Summaries are contained in F. S. Regs., Part II. and the Staff Manual respectively. Title pages will be prepared in manuscript.

Hour, Date, Place	Summary of Events and Information	Remarks and references to Appendices
4 April 3/15 OUDERDOM. cont.	"G" 20. & 3. B. at billets for personnel of this unit. Granlscourt Rest Station to continue its work for the present. Lieut. E.P. Scott investigated a case of Typhoid Fever on adult civilian. Report on same sent to D.S.O. YPRES. Number of Patients admitted to hospital during week. 168.	
9.30 a.m. 5/4/15 OUDERDOM.	Received instructions to transfer hospital at OUDERDOM to 14 B Field Ambulance, & to proceed to billets arranged near HOOFGRAAF. Visited A.D.M.S.	
6/4/15 HOOFGRAAF.	Visited A.D.M.S. & received instructions to evacuate Patients from Convalescent Rest Station & large barn which Canadian marquees which had been borrowed.	
2/15 pm "	Attended Conference of O.C. of 2nd Division Field Ambulances in YPRES. Visited school called "Ypriana" at the Holy Family, 39 Rue des Sœurs, YPRES. They were disappointed by shell fire & very dirty. This Field Ambulance had orders from division to find accommodation for 2 corps in a hospital. The upper storey of the buildings to be used for the Personnel & the Ambulances. The regimental quarters for the Patients. Accommodation	W Currie Col. OC 2 Ambulance

WAR DIARY
or
INTELLIGENCE SUMMARY.
(Erase heading not required.)

Army Form C. 2118.

Hour, Date, Place	Summary of Events and Information	Remarks and references to Appendices
7/4/15 HOOFGRAAF.	O.C. & Senior Officers & Quartermaster visited	
	the lines of Holy family & observation rooms	
	for different purposes. Arrangements made for	
	parking motor for unloading lorries.	
4pm " 8/4/15	Visited A.D.M.S. & Sporters.	
6 noon 9/4/15	B" Section paraded & proceeded to YPRES South	
12.30pm "	transport under Major H.H.10.	
	"C" Section paraded & proceeded to YPRES.	
" 9.4.15 YPRES.	"A" Section paraded & proceeded to YPRES.	
" 10.4.15 "	Preparation of Hospital.	
	Hospital opened & Patients admitted.	
2.0pm 11.4.15 "	"C" Section paraded to collect wounded. Number	
	of patients admitted during week = 69.	
3.0pm 12.4.15 "	"A" Section paraded to collect wounded.	
2.0pm 13.4.15 "	"B" Section paraded to collect wounded.	
2.0pm 14.4.15 "	"C" Section paraded to collect wounded.	

WAR DIARY
or
INTELLIGENCE SUMMARY.
(Erase heading not required.)

Army Form C. 2118.

Instructions regarding War Diaries and Intelligence Summaries are contained in F.S. Regs., Part II. and the Staff Manual respectively. Title pages will be prepared in manuscript.

Hour, Date, Place	Summary of Events and Information	Remarks and references to Appendices
6.0 pm 15-4-15. YPRES	All Sections paraded to collect wounded.	
8.0 pm 16-4-15 "	"A" Section paraded to collect wounded.	
8.0 pm 17-4-15 "	"C" Section paraded to collect wounded.	
" 18-4-15 "	Patients admitted during week 351.	
8.0 pm " 19-4-15 "	"B" Section paraded to collect wounded.	
8.0 pm " "	"A" Section paraded to collect wounded.	
8.0 pm " 20-4-15 "	Several shells fired into town.	
	Town heavily shelled by enemy. Two nuns of convent injured.	
7.0 pm "	"B" Section paraded to collect wounded.	
1.10 am 21-4-15 "	Received orders to evacuate hospital.	
10.0 am " "	"A" Section paraded to collect wounded from Lisse Inch, & assist the 14th Field Ambulance	
12.0 noon " "	Remains of unit paraded & proceeded to farm bivouac G.H.Q. 2.9.	
6.0 pm 22-4-15 POPERINGHE E.	"C" Section paraded to collect wounded.	
6.0 am 23-4-15 "	Begun admitting much & stands & Sergt Bell, both of whom had been wounded.	
" " "	A.D.M.S. and D.A.D.M.S. visited	
4.0 pm " "	"A" Section paraded to collect wounded.	

Army Form C. 2118.

WAR DIARY
or
INTELLIGENCE SUMMARY.
(Erase heading not required.)

Instructions regarding War Diaries and Intelligence Summaries are contained in F.S. Regs., Part II. and the Staff Manual respectively. Title pages will be prepared in manuscript.

Hour, Date, Place	Summary of Events and Information	Remarks and references to Appendices
6.0 pm. 24.4.15. POPERINGHE.	"B" Section heavy Canadian (2 sitting wounded, three sitting wounded wagon moderately (LAWTHER) wounded at Advanced Dressing Station	
6.0 pm " 25.4.15. "	Three ambulance drivers returned and reported ambulance wagon had been left at Advanced Dressing Station. Papers obtained to hospital during week. 233.	
6.0 am. 26.4.15. "	"C" Section Heavies Canadian to collect wounded. Heavies returned never seen INCH & reported 7/3 godn ambulance to be broken down, wagon mostly HALL and Privates TOMLINSON and FOTHERGILL killed, Privates PRATT and FALLS missing, Private CORRIGAN and driver DRABBLE wounded.	
8pm " "	(illegible)	
4.0 pm 27.4.15. "	Conference A.D.M.S., D.A.D.M.S., O.C. 2nd 2 Field Amb. O.C. 3rd Field Amb, and O.C. 96th Field Amb.	
6.0 pm " "	"B" Section Heavies Canadian to collect wounded.	
11.0 am 27.4.15. "	Burial of HALL and TOMLINSON whose bodies had been recovered during previous night.	
4.0 pm " "	Visit of A.D.M.S. and Lieut DRAYCOTT.	
6.0 pm " "	"C" Section Heavies Canadian to collect wounded.	

Army Form C. 2118.

WAR DIARY
or
INTELLIGENCE SUMMARY.
(Erase heading not required.)

Instructions regarding War Diaries and Intelligence Summaries are contained in F.S. Regs., Part II. and the Staff Manual respectively. Title pages will be prepared in manuscript.

Hour, Date, Place	Summary of Events and Information	Remarks and references to Appendices
4.0pm 29-4-15 POPERINGHE 6.0pm	Conference of A.D.M.S. and O.C.s of Fields Ambulances "A" Section Bearers Paraded for medical inspection. CAPT. ELLIS and LT. WILSON proceeded to POTIZE to take over advanced dressing station from 3rd LONDON FIELD AMBULANCE. Field Park and 4 PRES—ZONNEBEKE to be evacuated by 86th FIELD AMBULANCE. 129 patients collected. 3 stretchers wheels delivered at ZONNEBEKE for use of Bearers	
30 4/15 " "	Conference of A.D.M.S + O.Cs of 3 Field Ambulances of Division. 2 Bearers wounded and 3 not yet accounted for. Lt. INGH and Staff remained in Dug-outs of CHESHIRES all day with wounded who were not able to be removed before daylight. No 3 Motor Ambulance left on way near POTIZE Dressing station wth broken axle. In the stationary it had run into a newly-formed shell hole in the road. Cannot be recovered. No 2 Motor Ambulance had front hub & axle bt was able to proceed backwards for repairs. [Later Motor Ambulance & moving orders 3]	[signature] O.C. F6 Field Ambulance 2nd Northumbrian 2nd line

121/5/10
May 1915
S1

28th Division

86th (2nd Northumbrian) Field Ambulance

Vol IV

131/56/10

Army Form C. 2118.

WAR DIARY
or
INTELLIGENCE SUMMARY.
(Erase heading not required.)

2ND NORTHUMBRIAN FIELD AMBULANCE,
ROYAL ARMY MEDICAL CORPS. (T.F.)
(N.2 Field Amby)

Instructions regarding War Diaries and Intelligence Summaries are contained in F.S. Regs., Part II. and the Staff Manual respectively. Title pages will be prepared in manuscript.

Hour, Date, Place		Summary of Events and Information	Remarks and references to Appendices
Farm near to			
4-0 pm 1-5-15 POPERINGHE.		A.D.M.S. visited. Conference at POPERINGHE Junction.	
6-0 pm 1-5-15 "		"C" Section Bearers to collect wounded.	
		Motor Ambulances in Workshop - 2. 1 with broken stud about which wounds with wounded. CHESHIRES Depots became busy & unable to wounded and cleared.	
6-0 pm 2-5-15 "		"A" Section Bearers paraded to collect wounded. Motor ambulances in Workshop - 1.	
9-0 am 3-5-15 "		Unit paraded and proceeded to farm situated L29d. Sheet 27.	
6-0 pm 4-5-15 "		"A" Section Bearers paraded to collect wounded.	
12.30 pm 5-5-15 "		Unit paraded and proceeded to farm situated L.31.b. Sheet 24.	
7-0 pm 5-5-15 "		"B" Section Bearers paraded to collect wounded.	

Forms/C. 2118/10

Army Form C. 2118.

WAR DIARY

or

INTELLIGENCE SUMMARY.

(Erase heading not required.)

2ND NORTHUMBRIAN FIELD AMBULANCE,
ROYAL ARMY MEDICAL CORPS, (T.F.)
(2nd Field Amb.)

Hour, Date, Place	Summary of Events and Information	Remarks and references to Appendices
from rear to 6-0pm 6-5-15 POPERINGHE	"C" Section Bearers paraded to collect wounded. Motor Ambulances in Workshop 1.	
7-5-15 "	"A" Section Bearers paraded to collect wounded	
8-5-15 "	"B" Section Bearers paraded to collect wounded	
9-5-15 "	Pte Mitchell & Pte Murphy wounded.	
9-5-15 "	"C" Section Bearers paraded to collect wounded. Motor Ambulances in Workshop 2.	

COMMANDG 2 NORTHUMBRIAN FIELD
AMBULANCE R.A.M.C. (T.F.)
2nd Field Amb.
LIEUT. COLONEL

Army Form C. 2118.

WAR DIARY
or
INTELLIGENCE SUMMARY.
(Erase heading not required.)

2ND NORTHUMBRIAN FIELD AMBULANCE,
ROYAL ARMY MEDICAL CORPS. (T.F.)

Hour, Date, Place	Summary of Events and Information	Remarks and references to Appendices
10-5-15 From War to POPERINGHE	Motor Ambulances in Workshop - 3.	
11-5-15 5am. War to POPERINGHE	"A" Section Bearers paraded to collect wounded. Motor Ambulances in Workshop - 2.	
2-0pm 12-5-15 "	"A" Section Tent Sub-division went to Ypres Advanced Dressing Station. Motor Ambulances in Workshop - 2.	
10-10am 14-5-15 "	Unit paraded and proceeded to Walton Farm K3d. Sheet 27. Motor Ambulances in Workshop 2.	

COMMANDG 2 NORTHUMBRIAN FIELD AMBULANCE R.A.M.C. (T.F.)
LIEUT. COLONEL

Army Form C. 2118.

WAR DIARY
or
INTELLIGENCE SUMMARY.
(Erase heading not required.)

2ND NORTHUMBRIAN FIELD AMBULANCE,
ROYAL ARMY MEDICAL CORPS, (T.F.)
(1st Field Amb.)

Instructions regarding War Diaries and Intelligence Summaries are contained in F.S. Regs., Part II. and the Staff Manual respectively. Title pages will be prepared in manuscript.

Hour, Date, Place	Summary of Events and Information	Remarks and references to Appendices
10-5-15 WATOU (from rest to)	Motor Ambulances in Workshop 2.	
13-5-15 WATOU (from rest to)		
16-5-15 WATOU	"B" Section Tent Sub-division opened hospital at HOUTKERQUE. Sergt WHEATLEY and three men. Major HAIG, Lieut INCH, and Lieut SCOTT left on leave. Patients admitted to hospital - 6. / Motor Ambulances in Workshop - 2. Patients admitted to hospital - 16. / Motor Ambulances in Workshop - 2.	
17-5-15 " "		
18-5-15 " "	Lieut. WILSON temporarily attached to 3rd Royal Fusiliers. Lieut. BROWN temporarily attached to 2nd Royal Fusiliers. Lieut. ROBERTS temporarily attached to 1st Welsh Regt. Sergt CLARK took over hospital at HOUTKERQUE. Patients admitted to hospital - 39. / Motor Ambulances in Workshop - 2.	

(9 29 6) W 4141—463 100,000 9/14 HWV Forms/C. 2118/10

Army Form C. 2118.

WAR DIARY
or
INTELLIGENCE SUMMARY.
(Erase heading not required.)

2ND NORTHUMBRIAN FIELD AMBULANCE,
ROYAL ARMY MEDICAL CORPS. (T.F.)

Instructions regarding War Diaries and Intelligence Summaries are contained in F.S. Regs., Part II. and the Staff Manual respectively. Title pages will be prepared in manuscript.

Hour, Date, Place	Summary of Events and Information	Remarks and references to Appendices
10-0am 19-5-15 Farm near WATOU.	Unit paraded and proceeded to HERZEELE. Capt. ELLIS temporarily attached to 2nd East Surrey Regt. BRANDHOEK. Patients admitted to hospital - 2. Motor Ambulances in Workshop - 3.	Farm D.17c. Sheet 27.
20-5-15 Farm near HERZEELE	Hospital in HOUTKERQUE closed. Hospital opened at Chateau in HERZEELE. Sergt. WHEATLEY and four men. Patients admitted to hospital - 12. Motor Ambulances in Workshop 3.	Sergt. CLARK
21-5-15 " "	Capt. ELLIS returned to Unit. Lieut. WILSON returned to Unit. Lieut. BROWN returned to Unit. Patients admitted to hospital - 17. Motor Ambulances in Workshop - 2.	

Army Form C. 2118.

WAR DIARY
or
INTELLIGENCE SUMMARY.
(Erase heading not required.)

2ND NORTHUMBRIAN FIELD AMBULANCE,
ROYAL ARMY MEDICAL CORPS. (T.F.)
(2nd Field Amb.)

Instructions regarding War Diaries and Intelligence Summaries are contained in F.S. Regs., Part II. and the Staff Manual respectively. Title pages will be prepared in manuscript.

Hour, Date, Place	Summary of Events and Information	Remarks and references to Appendices
From rear to 22-5-15 HERZEELE	Patient admitted to hospital - 16.	
22-5-15 HERZEELE.	Hospital in HERZEELE closed and patient evacuated to 85th Area Ambulance. Workshop - 4. Motor Ambulances ed - Major HAIG, Lieut SCOTT and Lieut INCH returned from leave. Lieut BROWN temporarily attached to 2nd Cheshire Regt in place of Capt McEWAN sick.	
1-30 pm 22-5-15 From rear to BOESCHEPPE	Unit paraded and proceeded to farm situated L 34 c Shut 27. on BOESCHEPPE ROAD near POPERINGHE.	
7-0 pm 22-5-15 POPERINGHE	Sergt CLARK, Sergt BELL and four men paraded to collect wounded. Lieut WILSON & Lieut SCOTT in charge	

(B 29 6) W 4111—463   100,000   9/14   H W V   Forms/C. 2118/10

Army Form C. 2118.

2ND NORTHUMBRIAN FIELD AMBULANCE,
ROYAL ARMY MEDICAL CORPS. (T.F.)

WAR DIARY
or
INTELLIGENCE SUMMARY.
(Erase heading not required.)

Hour, Date, Place	Summary of Events and Information	Remarks and references to Appendices
From 23-5-15 to 7-0pm 23-5-15 POPERINGHE	Sergt LAWTON, Corpl ANDERSON and four men paraded to collect wounded. Lieut INCH and Lieut ROBERTS in charge. Motor Ambulances in Workshop – 4.	
7-0pm 24-5-15 "	Sergt SWALES and forty bearers paraded to collect wounded at WHITE CHATEAU and along MENIN ROAD. Bugler T. DAVEY killed and Pte. W. WOODCOCK wounded. Motor Ambulances in Workshop – 3.	
25-5-15 "	Major COULSTON visited and inspected Motor Ambulances of this Unit. Bugler T. DAVEY buried by Rev. Capt F. SCOTT, C.E. Chaplain. Full parade attended.	
4-0pm 25-5-15 "	Attended conference at Town Hall POPERINGHE, presided over by A.D.M.S. Diagnosis and treatment of poisonous gas.	

Army Form C. 2118.

WAR DIARY
or
INTELLIGENCE SUMMARY.
(Erase heading not required.)

2ND NORTHUMBRIAN FIELD AMBULANCE
ROYAL ARMY MEDICAL CORPS (T.F.)

Instructions regarding War Diaries and Intelligence Summaries are contained in F.S. Regs, Part II. and the Staff Manual respectively. Title pages will be prepared in manuscript.

Hour, Date, Place	Summary of Events and Information	Remarks and references to Appendices
6.0 pm 25-5-15 POPERINGHE	Sergt LAWTON and twenty men paraded to collect wounded.	
9.30 pm 25-5-15 "	Sergt BELL and sixty men paraded to collect wounded. Motor ambulances in Workshop 3.	
7.15 pm 26-5-15 "	Sergt ELLISON and forty men paraded to collect wounded. Lieut WILSON and Lieut INCH in charge.	
4.0 pm 26-5-15 "	Attended Conference at Town Hall POPERINGHE re Asphyxiating Gases. Motor ambulances in Workshop 4. Two motor ambulances temporarily attached.	
27-5-15 "	Lieut SCOTT temporarily attached to Northumbrian R.F.A. and returned to Unit same day. Lieut McINTYRE attached to Northumbrian R.F.A. Lieut KERR and Lieut QUINN attached. Motor ambulances in Workshop - 3.	

(9 29 6) W 41141–463 100,000 9/14 H W V Forms/C. 2118/10

Army Form C. 2118.

WAR DIARY
or
INTELLIGENCE SUMMARY.
(Erase heading not required.)

2ND NORTHUMBRIAN FIELD AMBULANCE,
ROYAL ARMY MEDICAL CORPS. (T.F.)
(86 Field Amb.)

Instructions regarding War Diaries and Intelligence Summaries are contained in F.S. Regs., Part II. and the Staff Manual respectively. Title pages will be prepared in manuscript.

Hour, Date, Place	Summary of Events and Information	Remarks and references to Appendices
4.0pm 27.5.15 POPERINGHE.	From Mar 6 to POPERINGHE. Attended Conference at Town Hall POPERINGHE re asphyxiating gases.	
7.15pm 27.5.15 "	Sergt CLARK, Sergt BELL and forty men paraded to collect wounded. Lieut ROBERTS & Lieut WILSON in charge.	
4.0pm 28.5.15 "	Attended Conference at Town Hall POPERINGHE by A.D.M.S. re instructions to new Field Ambulances in reference to evacuating wounded East of Ypres.	
7.30pm 28.5.15 "	Six men paraded to collect wounded. Lieut ROBERTS and Lieut INCH in charge. Lieut KERR attached to 63rd Brigade R.F.A. Lieut QUINN attached to 1st Welsh Regiment. Motor Ambulances in Workshops - 3.	
29.5.15 "	Lieut A.C.S. Smith attached.	
4.0pm 29.5.15 "	Attended conference at Town Hall POPERINGHE	
11.0am 29.5.15 "	Unit paraded and supplied with respirators for use against asphyxiating gases.	

Army Form C. 2118.

WAR DIARY
or
INTELLIGENCE SUMMARY.
(Erase heading not required.)

2ND NORTHUMBRIAN FIELD AMBULANCE,
ROYAL ARMY MEDICAL CORPS. (T.F.)

Instructions regarding War Diaries and Intelligence Summaries are contained in F.S. Regs., Part II. and the Staff Manual respectively. Title pages will be prepared in manuscript.

Hour, Date, Place	Summary of Events and Information	Remarks and references to Appendices
9am par to 29-5-15 A POPERINGHE	Motor Ambulances in Workshop - 2.	
10·0 am 30-5-15 A POPERINGHE	Unit paraded and proceeded to WATOU. Farm situated K3a. Sheet 27. Motor Ambulances in Workshop - 3	
10·0 am 31-5-15 A WATOU. Farm near to	Unit paraded for instructions regarding use of respirators. Visit from A.D.M.S.	
2-30 pm 31-5-15 " "	Motor Ambulances in Workshop - 4.	

COMMANDG 2 NORTHUMBRIAN FIELD
AMBULANCE R.A.M.C. (T.F.)
LIEUT. COLONEL

121/5875

107/5875

28th Division

86th Field Ambulance
6
Vol I

June 1915

Army Form C. 2118.

WAR DIARY
INTELLIGENCE SUMMARY.
(Erase heading not required.)

Instructions regarding War Diaries and Intelligence Summaries are contained in F. S. Regs., Part II and the Staff Manual respectively. Title pages will be prepared in manuscript.

Hour, Date, Place	Summary of Events and Information	Remarks and references to Appendices
1-6-15 farm near WATOU.	Hospital in HOUTKERQUE opened by "C" Section Tent Sub division.	
" "	Major FISHER and Lieut WILSON left on leave.	
" "	Lieut A.C.SMITH temporarily attached to R.E.	
" "	Patients in hospital 3	
" "	Cars in Running Order 4	
" "	" " Workshop 3.	
11-0am 2-6-15 " "	Inspection of grooming and saddlery by Lieut BROWELL Surrey Yeomanry in connection with sports held in honor of	
2-0pm " "	Sports. Kirk Natton.	
" "	Two cases suspected typhoid admitted to hospital in WATOU	
" "	Cars in Running Order 3	
" "	" " Workshop 4.	
" "	Patients in hospital 6.	

Army Form C. 2118.

WAR DIARY
INTELLIGENCE SUMMARY.
(Erase heading not required.)

Instructions regarding War Diaries and Intelligence Summaries are contained in F. S. Regs., Part II and the Staff Manual respectively. Title pages will be prepared in manuscript.

Hour, Date, Place	Summary of Events and Information	Remarks and references to Appendices
3-6-15 Farm near WATOU	Capt. ELLIS with 'A' Tent Subdivision took over hospital from Major HAIG and 'B' Tent Subdivision.	
" "	Lieut. FERENS in charge of a Motor Ambulance visited Headquarters of 83rd Brigade to collect three sick, but owing to incorrect geographical position he was unable to find them. On making enquiry at Divisional Headquarters was informed that this Brigade moved at 1·30 p.m. to WINNEZEELE.	
" "	Lieut. FERENS left on leave.	
" "	Visited 2nd Brigade R.F.A. re Medical and Sanitary arrangements.	
" "	Colonel RUNDLE. R.F.A. received into hospital.	
" "	Cars in Running Order 4.	
" "	" " Workshop 3	
" "	Patients in hospital 6.	
4-6-15	A.D.M.S. visited hospital and expressed himself satisfied with arrangements.	
" "	Visited R.E. re medical arrangements and Sanitation.	

COMMANDS 2 NORTHUMBRIAN FIELD AMBULANCE R.A.M.C. (T.F.)
LIEUT. COLONEL

Army Form C. 2118.

WAR DIARY
or
INTELLIGENCE SUMMARY.
(Erase heading not required.)

Instructions regarding War Diaries and Intelligence Summaries are contained in F.S. Regs., Part II and the Staff Manual respectively. Title pages will be prepared in manuscript.

Hour, Date, Place	Summary of Events and Information	Remarks and references to Appendices
4-6-15 Farm near WATOU.	Cyclist Orderly sent for duty at A.D.M.S. Office.	
" "	Cars in Running Order 4.	
" "	" " Workshop 3.	
" "	Patients in hospital. 30.	
" "	Two cases suspected typhoid sent to C.C.S. HAZEBROUCK.	
5-6-15 "	Visited Howitzer Brigade re Sanitation and Medical arrangements.	
" "	Received instructions to pitch Camp hospital of 36 Bell Tents in field of farm on which we are billeted.	
" "	A.D.M.S. inspected Camp and Camp hospital.	
" "	Cars in Running Order 5	
" "	" " Workshop 2	
" "	Patients in hospital 31.	
6-6-15 "	General BULFIN and A.D.M.S. visited Camp. General BULFIN expressed himself pleased with work of Unit in this country and was satisfied with arrangements of Camp hospital.	

Army Form C. 2118.

WAR DIARY
INTELLIGENCE SUMMARY.
(Erase heading not required.)

Instructions regarding War Diaries and Intelligence Summaries are contained in F.S. Regs., Part II and the Staff Manual respectively. Title pages will be prepared in manuscript.

Hour, Date, Place			Summary of Events and Information	Remarks and references to Appendices
6pm.	6-6-15.	Ferme près WATOU.	Ten N.C.Os and men left on leave	
	"	"	Major FISHER and Lieut. WILSON returned from leave.	
	"	"	Lieut. INCH went to A.D.M.S. Office for duty.	
	"	"	Cars in Running Order 4.	
	"	"	" " Workshop 3.	
	"	"	Patients in Hospital 62.	
	7-6-15	"	Capt. ELLIS and Lieut. ROBERTS left on leave.	
	"	"	Major FISHER took charge of hospital in WATOU.	
	"	"	Cars in Running Order 5.	
	"	"	" " Workshop 2.	
	"	"	Patients in hospital 61.	
	"	"	O.C. left on leave.	
6am	8-6-15	"	Major HAIG visited Divisional Cyclists, Surrey Yeomanry, 3rd Brigade R.F.A, and Headquarters Coy. Divisional Train. A.S.C re sanitary arrangements.	
	"	"	Lieut LYALL left on leave.	

Army Form C. 2118.

WAR DIARY
INTELLIGENCE SUMMARY.
(Erase heading not required.)

Instructions regarding War Diaries and Intelligence Summaries are contained in F.S. Regs., Part II. and the Staff Manual respectively. Title pages will be prepared in manuscript.

Hour, Date, Place	Summary of Events and Information	Remarks and references to Appendices
8-6-15. 1pm near WATOU.	Major HAIG visited A.D.M.S. and got instructions re Sanitary arrangements 85th Brigade Area. Two cases suspected typhoid sent to C.C.S. HAZEBROUCK. Cars in Running Order 5. " " Workshop 2. Patients in Hospital 57.	
9-6-15	Lieut FERENS returned from leave. Major HAIG inspected Sanitary arrangements of 2nd Buffs 2nd East Surreys, 3rd Royal Fusiliers, 3rd Middlesex and 8th Middlesex. Lieut DEIGHTON R.A.M.C. arrived. Major HAIG visited A.D.M.S. to report and received instructions to inspect Water Carts of 85th Brigade. Cars in Running Order 4. " " Workshop 3. Patients in Hospital 87.	

WAR DIARY
INTELLIGENCE SUMMARY.
(Erase heading not required.)

Army Form C. 2118.

Hour, Date, Place	Summary of Events and Information	Remarks and references to Appendices
10-6-15. 2pm near WATOU	Major HAIG inspected Water Carts of Battalions composing 85th Brigade.	
" " "	Lieut DEIGHTON attached to 5th K.O.R.L. Regiment.	
" " "	Two cases suspected typhoid sent to C.C.S. HAZEBROUCK.	
" " "	Cars in Running Order 4	
" " "	" " Workshop 3.	
" " "	Patients in hospital. 93.	
11-6-15 "	Ten N.C.O's and men returned from leave	
" "	Cars in Running Order. 5	
" "	" " Workshop. 2	
" "	Patients in hospital. 101.	
12-6-15 "	O.C. returned from leave.	
" "	Capt. ELLIS and Lieut. ROBERTS returned from leave	
" "	Cars in Running Order 5.	
" "	" " Workshop 2.	
" "	Patients in hospital 108.	

Commands 2 Northumbrian Field Ambulance R.A.M.C. (T.F)
Lieut. Colonel

Army Form C. 2118.

WAR DIARY
INTELLIGENCE SUMMARY.
(Erase heading not required.)

Instructions regarding War Diaries and Intelligence Summaries are contained in F.S. Regs., Part II and the Staff Manual respectively. Title pages will be prepared in manuscript.

Hour, Date, Place	Summary of Events and Information	Remarks and references to Appendices
13-6-15 Summer WATOU.	Lieut LYALL returned from leave.	
" "	Visited Field Ambulance at LA CLYTTE and DICKEBUSCHE (with ADMS)	
" "	Lieut MITCHELL joined 3rd Madhurs in place of Lieut KNOWLES.	
" "	Lieut INCH returned to Unit.	
" "	Lieut SMITH went to A.D.M.S. 4th Division for duty. Received orders to remain at WATOU and to send two Motor Ambulances to 84th Field Ambulance at LA CLYTTE for temporary duty.	
" "	Three Horse Ambulance Wagons accompanied 83rd Brigade to pick up men fallen out on march between WINEZEELE and WESTOUTRE.	
" "	Cars in Running Order 5 " " Workshop 2	
" "	Motor Cycle broken down at STEENVOORDE. Patient in hospital 123.	

Commdg 2 Northumbrian Field Ambulance R.A.M.C. (T.F.)
Lieut. Colonel

Army Form C. 2118.

WAR DIARY
of
INTELLIGENCE SUMMARY.
(Erase heading not required.)

Instructions regarding War Diaries and Intelligence Summaries are contained in F. S. Regs., Part II. and the Staff Manual respectively. Title pages will be prepared in manuscript.

Hour, Date, Place		Summary of Events and Information	Remarks and references to Appendices
14-6-15	9am WATOU	A.D.M.S. visited Camp and hospital.	
"	"	A.D.M.S. Office removed from WATOU to WESTOUTRE	
"	"	Cars in Running Order 5	
"	"	" " Workshop 2	
"	"	Patients in hospital 128	
"	"	6 Reinforcement joined.	
15-6-15	"	Three cases suspected typhoid sent to C.C.S. HAZEBROUCK.	
"	"	Cars in Running order 5.	
"	"	" " Workshop 2	
"	"	Patients in hospital 133.	
16-6-15	"	Cars in Running Order 4	
"	"	" " Workshop 3	
"	"	Motor Cycle in Workshop.	
"	"	Patients in hospital 147.	

COMMANDG 2 NORTHUMBRIAN FIELD AMBULANCE R.A.M.C. (T.F.)
LIEUT. COLONEL

Army Form C. 2118.

WAR DIARY
INTELLIGENCE SUMMARY.
(Erase heading not required.)

Instructions regarding War Diaries and Intelligence Summaries are contained in F.S. Regs., Part II. and the Staff Manual respectively. Title pages will be prepared in manuscript.

Hour, Date, Place	Summary of Events and Information	Remarks and references to Appendices
17-6-15 Farm near WATOU.	Cars in Running Order 4.	
" " "	" " Workshop 3.	
" " "	Patients in hospital 156.	
18-6-15 "	Cars in Running Order 4.	
" " "	" " Workshop 3.	
" " "	Patients in hospital 167.	
19-6-15 "	Lieuts SCOTT and ROBERTS sent to 84th Field Ambulance for temporary duty.	
" " "	Major HAIG went to ROUEN for duty.	
" " "	Lieuts TAYLOR and MELLOR 3rd Royal Fusiliers Medically examined passed fit for Repairs	
" " "	One case suspected typhoid sent to C.C.S. HAZEBROUCK.	
" " "	Cars in Running Order. 5.	
" " "	" " Workshop 2.	
" " "	Patients in hospital 179.	

COMMANDS 2 NORTH'N FIELD AMBULANCE R.A.M.C. (T.F.)
LIEUT COLONEL

Army Form C. 2118.

WAR DIARY
or
INTELLIGENCE SUMMARY.
(Erase heading not required.)

Instructions regarding War Diaries and Intelligence Summaries are contained in F.S. Regs., Part II and the Staff Manual respectively. Title pages will be prepared in manuscript.

Hour, Date, Place	Summary of Events and Information	Remarks and references to Appendices
6pm. 20-6-15 Farm near WATOU	Unit paraded and marched to farm near BOESCHEPE situated R15.b. sheet 27 1/40,000, via STEENVOORDE and GODEWAERSVELDE, to avoid Brigade troops marching in same district. No men or horses fell out on march. Capt. ELLIS and a tent sub division with transport and Motor Ambulances, remained behind at WATOU. Cars in Working Order 5. " " " Workshop 2. Patients evacuated to C.C.S. 8. " " " Mont-des-Cats 196. " " " to duty 10.	
21-6-15 Farm near BOESCHEPE	A.D.M.S. visited Camp. Hospital in WATOU closed. Capt. ELLIS with a Tent Sub-division, transport and Motor Ambulances joined Unit. Hospital Camp with accommodation for 38 patients pitched. Water supply for drinking purposes had to be drawn from a Well, guarded, ½ a mile away. Water for ablution purposes drawn from spring in Camp. Hospital field, and for personnel from pump where personnel are bivouacked.	

(73869) W4141—463. 400,000. 9/14. H.&J.Ltd. Forms/C. 2118/10.

Army Form C. 2118.

WAR DIARY
or
INTELLIGENCE SUMMARY.
(Erase heading not required.)

Instructions regarding War Diaries and Intelligence Summaries are contained in F. S. Regs., Part II and the Staff Manual respectively. Title pages will be prepared in manuscript.

Hour, Date, Place	Summary of Events and Information	Remarks and references to Appendices
21-6-15 Summer BOESCHEPE	One Motor Ambulance Radiator and front axle damaged by car running down incline owing to brakes not holding. Cars in running Order 6 " " " " Workshop 1.	
22-6-15 " " "	Visited 3rd North Midland Field Ambulance, 46th Division the Musée at BAILLEUL, whose hospital we are to take over. Cars in Running Order 4 " " " Workshop 3.	
23-6-15 " " "	A.D.M.S. visited Camp. Visited Mont-dis-Cats, 2nd Army Rest Station, run by Midland Clearing hospital, also visited 1st (13th) Field Ambulance in BOESCHEPE. Three Planket wagons three pairs of horses and drivers sented to A.S.C. Cars in Running Order 5. 0" " Workshop 2. Patients in hospital 2.	

Army Form C. 2118.

WAR DIARY
INTELLIGENCE SUMMARY.
(Erase heading not required.)

Instructions regarding War Diaries and Intelligence Summaries are contained in F.S. Regs., Part II. and the Staff Manual respectively. Title pages will be prepared in manuscript.

Hour, Date, Place	Summary of Events and Information	Remarks and references to Appendices
24-6-15 Garrison BOESCHEPE	3rd North Midland Field Ambulance hospital in BAILLEUL taken over by Major FISHER and 44 N.C.Os and men.	
" "	Lieut ROBERTS returned to Unit.	
" "	Lieut ROBERTS went to BAILLEUL for duty at hospital.	
" "	Cars in running order 5.	
" "	" " Workshop 2.	
" "	Patients in hospital 1.	
25-6-15 "	Received from Red Cross Society various articles for use at hospital in BAILLEUL.	
" "	Major FISHER, Lieut WARDLE & Staff Sergt WEBSTER mentioned in Sir JOHN FRENCH'S despatch in "The Times" dated June 21st 1915.	
" "	Evacuated patients left by 3rd North Midland Field Ambulance at BAILLEUL hospital.	
" "	Visited Mont-des-Cats and arranged for 28th Division patients to be taken to our hospital.	

Signed LIEUT. COLONEL
COMMANDING 2 NORTHUMBRIAN
AMBULANCE R.A.M.C. (T.F.) FIELD

WAR DIARY
INTELLIGENCE SUMMARY.
(Erase heading not required.)

Army Form C. 2118.

Instructions regarding War Diaries and Intelligence Summaries are contained in F. S. Regs., Part II. and the Staff Manual respectively. Title pages will be prepared in manuscript.

Hour, Date, Place	Summary of Events and Information	Remarks and references to Appendices
25-6-15 Eecke nr BOESCHEPE	Cars in Running Order 5	
"	" " " Workshop 2	
"	Patients in hospital 49.	
"	Cyclist Messenger went to BAILLEUL hospital for duty.	
26-6-15 "	Three blanket wagons, three pairs horses and drivers returned to Unit from A.S.C.	
"	Water supply in BAILLEUL drawn between the hours of 7.30 + 10am and 2.30 and 5pm. and must be Chlorinated before use.	
"	Lieut WARDLE rejoined Unit.	
"	Six wooden beds with spring mattresses taken from the Asylum Ypres for use in hospital at BAILLEUL.	
"	16 Asylum Ypres for use in hospital in Hopside 56.	
27-6-15 "	Twenty beds taken from the Asylum Ypres for use in hospital at BAILLEUL.	
"	Colonel GEDDES DDMS. accompanied by ADMS visited Camp and Camp hospital.	

COMMANDG 2 NORTHUMBRIAN FIELD AMBULANCE R.A.M.C.
LIEUT. COLONEL

Army Form C. 2118.

WAR DIARY
of
INTELLIGENCE SUMMARY.
(Erase heading not required.)

Instructions regarding War Diaries and Intelligence Summaries are contained in F. S. Regs., Part II. and the Staff Manual respectively. Title pages will be prepared in manuscript.

Hour, Date, Place	Summary of Events and Information	Remarks and references to Appendices
27-6-15 Farm near BOESCHEPE	Cars in Running Order 6.	
" "	" " Workshop 1.	
" "	Patients in hospital 39.	
28-6-15 "	Ten badly damaged Beds and bedding, also several Tables and a chairs removed from the debris of the male asylum, Ypres for use in hospital. Six pairs of horses, one N.C.O and three drivers sent to BAILLEUL to the Town Major, Major LORD GASSELIS, for cleaning streets and other sanitary duties.	
" "	Cars in Running Order 6.	
" "	" " Workshop 1.	
" "	Patients in hospital 48.	
29-6-15 "	Cars in running order 6.	
" "	" " Workshop 1.	
" "	Patients in Hospital 64.	

WAR DIARY
INTELLIGENCE SUMMARY
(Erase heading not required.)

Army Form C. 2118.

Instructions regarding War Diaries and Intelligence Summaries are contained in F.S. Regs., Part II and the Staff Manual respectively. Title pages will be prepared in manuscript.

Hour, Date, Place	Summary of Events and Information	Remarks and references to Appendices
30/6/15 BOESCHEPE	Cars in Running Order 6. " " Workshop 1. Patients in hospital 103.	

COMMANDS 2 NORTHUMBRIAN FIELD AMBULANCE R.A.M.C. (T.F.)
LIEUT. COLONEL

121/6341

28th Division

12/6341

86th Field Ambulance

Vol VI

July 15.

Army Form C. 2118

WAR DIARY
INTELLIGENCE SUMMARY
(Erase heading not required.)

**2ND NORTHUMBRIAN FIELD AMBULANCE,
ROYAL ARMY MEDICAL CORPS. (T.F.)**

Instructions regarding War Diaries and Intelligence Summaries are contained in F.S. Regs., Part II and the Staff Manual respectively. Title Pages will be prepared in manuscript.

Place	Date	Hour	Summary of Events and Information	Remarks and references to Appendices
Same place BOESCHEPPE	1-7-15		A.D.M.S. 26th Division visited and inspected minutely every section of Camp and Camp Hospital and Grouzpous Section.	DK
			Patients in Hospital 101.	
			Cars on running orders 6	
			" " Workshop 1.	
" "	2-7-15		Visited section Hospital at BAILLEUL.	
			Lieut ROBERTS, D.R.2 returned by Lieut SCOTT, R.T.	
			R.C. Chaplain CARLISLE attached 86th Field Ambulance.	
			Patients in Hospital 120.	
			Cars on running orders 6 - Cars in Workshop 1.	
" "	3-7-15		Received orders from D.D.M.S. II Corps that the sick belonging to 2nd Corps are to be attended to by nearest Field Ambulance including the Hospital at BAILLEUL.	
			Lieut WARDLE, V.H. directed as additional Medical officer at Convalescent Rest Camp	
			Patients in Hospital 132.	
			Cars in running orders 6	
			" " Workshop 1.	

Sd/ [signature]
LIEUT. COLONEL
**COMMANDG (2 NORTHUMBRIAN) FIELD
AMBULANCE R.A.M.C. (T.F.)**

Army Form C. 2118

WAR DIARY
or
INTELLIGENCE SUMMARY
(Erase heading not required.)

Instructions regarding War Diaries and Intelligence Summaries are contained in F. S. Regs., Part II. and the Staff Manual respectively. Title Pages will be prepared in manuscript.

Place	Date	Hour	Summary of Events and Information	Remarks and references to Appendices
From rest BOESINGHE	4.7.15		MAJOR-GENERAL BULFIN, ES, CVO, C.B. visited Camp and Canp Hospital, accompanied by A.D.M.S. 28 Division. Patients in Hospital 159. Cars in running order 6. " " Workshop 1.	
" "	5.7.15		Visited Section Hospital at BAILLEUL. Patients in Hospital 162. Cars in running order 6. " " Workshop 1.	
" "	6.7.15		Received orders from A.D.M.S. 28 Division to reequip patients fit for duty with equipment of men who will not be fit for duty in 14 days and men who are likely to be sent to Casualty Clearing Station. Th Section running Hospital at BAILLEUL is to arrange for Dental treatment for patients by Dental Surgeon of No 3 Casualty Clearing Station. Patients in Hospital 154.	

2nd NORTHUMBRIAN FIELD AMBULANCE
ROYAL ARMY MEDICAL CORPS.

WAR DIARY or INTELLIGENCE SUMMARY

Army Form C. 2118

(Erase heading not required.)

Place	Date	Hour	Summary of Events and Information	Remarks and references to Appendices
Convent near BOESCHEPE	4/1/15		Patients evacuated from Section Hospital at BAILLEUL. Patients in Hospital 186. Cases on morning orders 6. " " Workshop 1.	
"	5/1/15		3. C.S. wagons with equipment from BAILLEUL. 56th Field Ambulance to form Divisional Rest Station only. Patients in Hospital 70. Cases on morning orders 6. " " Workshop 1.	
"	7/1/15		Conference of O/C's Field Ambulances 28 Division at office of A.D.M.S. 28th Division at WESTOUTRE in reference to arrangement of work of Field Ambulances no more each was to have a section of trenches from which evacuation of wounded was to take place. Several resolutions to go over ground where Aid Posts and Dressing Stations were to be chosen. MAJOR DL FISHER and 4 N.C.O's and men returned to camp from BAILLEUL Hospital. Patients in Hospital 95. Cases on morning orders 6. " " Workshop 1.	

J. W. [signature]
O.C. 2nd Northumbrian Field Ambulance
Royal Army Medical Corps (T.F.)

WAR DIARY OF INTELLIGENCE SUMMARY

(Erase heading not required.)

Army Form C. 2118

Place	Date	Hour	Summary of Events and Information	Remarks and references to Appendices
Farm near BOESCHEPE	10/7/15		With A.D.M.S. 28th Division and O.C. Field Ambulance motored over areas chosen previous day and also Aid Posts of areas and prospective sites for Dressing Stations and fields for Detachment's Bearers. With A.D.M.S. 28th Division called on BRIGADIER GENERAL H.S.L. RAVENSHAW. C.M.G. G.O.C. 83rd Brigade 28 Division who indicated the position in which he preferred should be situated Dressing Station and which was to be rendezvous for Motor Ambulances. Patients in Hospital 110. Cars in running order 6. " " Workshop 1.	
"	11/7/15		With A.D.M.S., D.A.D.M.S. 28 Division and MAJOR MONTGOMERY-SMITH 84th Field Ambulance motored over areas which had been allocated to a section of Field Ambulances. Patients in Hospital 161. Cars in running order 6. " Workshop 1.	
"	12/7/15		Detailed "B" Section under Capt. E.R. ELLIS together with LIEUTS E.P. SCOTT and D.R.E. ROBERTS to occupy billets on farm near N.I.C.8.8. from West Section & Bearer posted under N.C.O. no details to a billet on farm behind aid of KEMMEL BANK and to there form a Rendezvous from which they may be able to other Bearers from Aid Posts of 83rd Brigade and from which they can send out Bearers as required From today out Field Ambulance so posted to evacuate Head posts and sent empty and eliminated of 83rd Brigade to 84 Field Ambulance Dressing Station at LACLYTTE	

8th (2nd NORTHUMBRIAN) FIELD AMBULANCE (T.F.)
ROYAL ARMY MEDICAL CORPS.

WAR DIARY
or
INTELLIGENCE SUMMARY

(Erase heading not required.)

Army Form C. 2118

Instructions regarding War Diaries and Intelligence Summaries are contained in F. S. Regs., Part II. and the Staff Manual respectively. Title Pages will be prepared in manuscript.

Place	Date	Hour	Summary of Events and Information	Remarks and references to Appendices
Ferme Nieppe Bois de Ploegsteert	12/4/15		2 Horse Ambulances sent back "B" Section this day. Moved out with Capt Ellis to show him ground which B Section are to occupy and gave him directions on the spot.	
		9 a.m.	Sick Rpt: 5 a.m. arrived 10 a.m. Patients in Hospital 188. Care in running order 6. " Workshop 1.	
"	13/4/15		Patients in Hospital 174. Care in running order 6. " Workshop 1.	
"	14/4/15		Inspected Med Rec. H.Q. (Hazebrouck) by Major Montgomery D.D.M.S. Attached Medical Officers at 84th Field Ambulance LA CLYTTE. Two men were found not to be in same as some of officers at which died by hand. 3rd MIDDLESEX R.E. #7. Patients in Hospital 156. Care in running order 6. " Workshop 1.	
"	15/4/15		Wire from A.D.M.S. 28th Division and 2nd Col. SHARP 85/1st Field Ambulance. Arranging taking over Hospital at LA CLYTTE from 84 Field Ambulance and handing our Divisional Rest Station BOESCHEPPE to Co 2 Amb. Patients in Hospital 156. Care in running order 6. " Workshop 1.	

86th (2ND NORTHUMBRIAN) FIELD AMBULANCE
ROYAL ARMY MEDICAL CORPS. (T.F.)

Army Form C. 2118

WAR DIARY
~~INTELLIGENCE SUMMARY~~
(Erase heading not required.)

Instructions regarding War Diaries and Intelligence Summaries are contained in F. S. Regs., Part II and the Staff Manual respectively. Title Pages will be prepared in manuscript.

Place	Date	Hour	Summary of Events and Information	Remarks and references to Appendices
From west BOESCHEPPE	16/7/15		"A" and "C" Sections together with transport section moved from Divisional Rest Station BOESCHEPPE to LACLYTTE.	
LACLYTTE		12:30p/m	Arrived at LACLYTTE.	
"			CAPT. G. R. ELLIS and party of men from "B" Section took over hospital from 5th Field Ambulance in mid morning.	
"			MAJOR D. W. FISHER and "C" Section took over hospital from CAPT. G. R. ELLIS.	
"			Saw Brigadier General 53rd Brigade who advised when Advd Dsg was. "B" Section Bearers paraded to collect wounded. Received ore wheeled carrier from 8th Field Ambulance and came to Advanced Dressing Station at KEMMEL.	
"			Patients in hospital 53.	
"			Cases on morning order 6 Mortality 1.	
"	17/7/15		"A" Section Bearers paraded to collect wounded. Patients in hospital 48 Cases in morning order 6 Mortality 1.	

J. Hunter
LIEUT. ~~COLONEL~~ FIELD
COMMAND[IN]G (2 NORTHUMBRIAN) (T.F.)
AMBULANCE R.A.M.C.
86 Full bnd

Army Form C. 2118

WAR DIARY
or
INTELLIGENCE SUMMARY
(Erase heading not required.)

Instructions regarding War Diaries and Intelligence Summaries are contained in F. S. Regs., Part II. and the Staff Manual respectively. Title Pages will be prepared in manuscript.

Place	Date	Hour	Summary of Events and Information	Remarks and references to Appendices
LA CLYTTE	18-7-15		Visit from A.D.M.S. and D.A.D.M.S. 25th Division who inspected Hospital and Billets of personnel. Surplus articles drawn from BRITISH RED CROSS SOCIETY sent to 84th Field Ambulance.	
"	19-7-15		"C" Section Bearers paraded to collect wounded. Patients in Hospital 39. Cars on running test 6. Motor lorries 1.	
"	"		"B" Section Bearers paraded to collect wounded. Patients in Hospital 35. Cars on running test 6. Motor lorries 1.	
"	20-7-15		A.D.M.S. 25 Division visited Hospital. "A" Section Bearers paraded to collect wounded. Patients in Hospital 35. Cars on running test 6. Motor lorries 1.	

[signature]
LIEUT. COLONEL
COMMANDG 2 NORTHUMBRIAN FIELD
AMBULANCE R.A.M.C. (T.F.)

Army Form C. 2118

WAR DIARY
or
INTELLIGENCE SUMMARY
(Erase heading not required.)

Instructions regarding War Diaries and Intelligence Summaries are contained in F. S. Regs., Part II. and the Staff Manual respectively. Title Pages will be prepared in manuscript.

Place	Date	Hour	Summary of Events and Information	Remarks and references to Appendices
LA CLYTTE	21.7.15		On instructions from A.D.M.S. 28th Division forwarded all unclaimed Kits, Rifles &c. via 2 G.S. Waggons to Ordnance Stores at RAILHEAD. Parties in attendance also paraded to collect wounded. H.Q. Section Bearers paraded to collect wounded. Cars in Running order & 1 Car in Workshop. Moved verbal instructions from G.O.C. 25th Division removed sick and wounded from Hospital at LA CLYTTE to Hospital adjoining - A and C Sections together with transport moved from LA CLYTTE to Hospital Field (M.9.0) WESTOUTRE. "B" Section reported that evening for the Sherwood Foresters Brigade. A.D.M.S. 28th Division verbally acquired to these instructions later in the day.	
		6 p.m.	Moved from LA CLYTTE. "B" Section together with kitchen and 2 Motor Ambulances detailed to proceed to KEMMEL to evacuate wounded.	
WESTOUTRE		7.0 p.m.	Arrived at Hospital Field M.9.0. and Bivouacked for night.	
	23.7.15		Received temporary Precedent Lt. Col. D'A ANZRON - thereafter MAJOR DE PITTEROND. CAPT GREFIELD reported CAPT BAMFORD for permanent transmission. CAPT CUMBERBATCH asked to G.O.C. 28th Division asked and obtained permission for the French interpreter Legroire to proceed the following day to St JANS CAPELLE to complete the engineering formalities of the states supply. LIEUT SCOTT E.P. handed over 2 Ariel foods on the KEMMEL-VIERSTRAAT ROAD. 85th Field Ambulance	

LIEUT. COLONEL
COMMANDG 2 NORTHUMBRIAN FIELD
AMBULANCE R.A.M.C. (T.F.)

1875 Wt. W593/826 1,000,000 4/15 J.B.C. & A. A.D.S.S./Forms/C. 2118.

WAR DIARY
of
INTELLIGENCE SUMMARY

(Erase heading not required.)

Army Form C. 2118

Instructions regarding War Diaries and Intelligence Summaries are contained in F.S. Regs., Part II. and the Staff Manual respectively. Title Pages will be prepared in manuscript.

Place	Date	Hour	Summary of Events and Information	Remarks and references to Appendices
WESTOUTRE	23-7-15 Contd		LIEUT ROBERTS. A.R.E. took over the Anor Post of the 84th BRIGADE which had been previously answered by 85th Field Ambulance. "B" Section Bearers parceded to collect wounded and closed them to 85th Field Ambulance.	
"	24-7-15		French Interpreter Legendre reported at Headquarters as Denickson to go to "B" Section CAPPELL South with reference to Water Supply.	
"	"	1.15 pm	"A" and "C" Sections together with transport moved from WESTOUTRE and marched to LOCRE. (3.45 pm)	
LOCRE	"	2 pm	Arrived LOCRE and took over Hospital at Convent SANTOINE from "A" section 55th Field Ambulance.	
			"B" Section Bearer Sub-Division was joined by request of that section which had been stationed at farm on KEMMEL BANK and in charge of LT E.P. SCOTT marched to LOCRE joining the remainder of their Ambulances at that place.	
			19 Sick and 1 wounded taken over from 85th Field Ambulance. 9469 Pte HOLLEX J. 1st Suffolk Regt died of wounds.	
			Two motor orders from A.D.M.S. 1 Horse Ambulance Wagon accompanied Regiment from WESTOUTRE to GODEWAMSVELOE to fetch up charges.	
			"C" Section Bearers paraded to collect wounded. Bearer Sub-divisions under Capt Sin working kept 1.	

1875 Wt. W593/826 1,000,000 4/15 J.B.C. & A. A.D.S.S./Forms/C. 2118.

COMMANDING 2 NORTHUMBRIAN FIELD AMBULANCE R.A.M.C. (T.F.)

LIEUT & C
86 F Ward

Army Form C. 2118

WAR DIARY
or
INTELLIGENCE SUMMARY
(Erase heading not required.)

Instructions regarding War Diaries and Intelligence Summaries are contained in F. S. Regs., Part II. and the Staff Manual respectively. Title Pages will be prepared in manuscript.

Place	Date	Hour	Summary of Events and Information	Remarks and references to Appendices
LOCRE	25.7.15		"A" Section Bearers paraded to collect wounded. Patients in Hospital 22. Cars on running order 6. " wounded 1.	
	26.7.15		D.A.D.M.S. 28th Division visited and inspected Hospital. Medical Board on fellow Presedent Lt.Col. D.A. CAMERON. Members MAJOR MONTGOMERY-SMITH and CAPT C.R. ELLIS. appointed to enquire into the state of mind of PTE LEWIS.W. 2 EAST SURREY REGT. Found man incapable of understanding military duties.... LIEUT. E.P. SCOTT detailed for temporary duty with 2nd Bn BUFFS REGT. "B" Section Bearers paraded to collect wounded. Patients in Hospital 36. Cars on running order 6. " " " " " " 1.	
	27.7.15		By verbal orders of A.D.M.S. 28 Division heard on Pte LEWIS.W. As consequence to enquire of this man was it was not a raving lunatic. He had decided he was not a raving lunatic and was therefore able to plead. A.D.M.S. 25 Division visited Hospital. "C" Section Bearers paraded to collect wounded. Patients in Hospital 44. Cars on running order 6. " " wounded "	

1875 Wt. W593/826 1,000,000 4/15 J.B.C. & A. A.D.S.S./Forms/C.2118.

LIEUT. COLONEL
COMMANDG (2 NORTHUMBRIAN) FIELD
AMBULANCE R.A.M.C. (T.F)
26 July 1915

Army Form C. 2118

WAR DIARY
INTELLIGENCE SUMMARY
(Erase heading not required.)

Instructions regarding War Diaries and Intelligence Summaries are contained in F. S. Regs., Part II. and the Staff Manual respectively. Title Pages will be prepared in manuscript.

Place	Date	Hour	Summary of Events and Information	Remarks and references to Appendices
LOCRE	26-7-15		A.D.M.S. & D.A.D.M.S. 28 Division visited and inspected Hospital. Col. GEDDES, D.D.M.S. II Corps visited and inspected Hospital and Billets.	
			A. Section Bearers paraded to collect wounded.	
			Patients in Hospital 33.	
			Cars in running order 7.	
"	29-7-15		"B" Section Bearers paraded to collect wounded.	
			Patients in Hospital 39.	
			Cars in running order 4.	
"	30-7-15		Colonel SIR JOHN BRADFORD of No.7 Stationary Hospital BOULOGNE called at Hospital to see two nephews LT MARSH-ROBERTS. As a result of visit instructions were received for GENERAL PORTER, D.M.S. 2nd Army through A.D.M.S. 28th Division that LT MARSH-ROBERTS would be evacuated to No.7 Stationary Hospital BOULOGNE. By arrangements made with LT. DRAYCOTT. No 15 Sanitary Section 28 Division the washing be required for the Hospital is done by the sisters of the Convent in which the Hospital is billeted.	
			"C" Section Bearers paraded to collect wounded.	
			Patients in Hospital 58.	
			Cars in running order 4.	

LIEUT. COLONEL
COMMANDING (2 NORTHUMBRIAN)
AMBULANCE R.A.M.C. (T.F.)

WAR DIARY
or
INTELLIGENCE SUMMARY

(Erase heading not required.)

Army Form C. 2118

Instructions regarding War Diaries and Intelligence Summaries are contained in F. S. Regs., Part II. and the Staff Manual respectively. Title Pages will be prepared in manuscript.

Place	Date	Hour	Summary of Events and Information	Remarks and references to Appendices
LOCRE	31/7/15		In accordance with instructions received Lt MARSH-ROBERTS transferred to No 9 Stationary Hospital BOULOGNE. MAJOR FISHER was detailed to accompany this Officer. During this morning between 7 and 9-30 o'clock 2 men of Belgian Nationality were noticed by S. Sergt PARKER 86 Field Ambulance acting in a very suspicious manner in the vicinity of a Heavy Battery of Artillery. Acting on above information was sent to the Officer in charge of the Battery, who instructed S. Sergt Parker and a man from the Battery to detain the men who were taken to 151st Brigade Headquarters R.G.A. The men were placed under a Guard and taken to LOCRE to the BELGIAN Officer in charge. This officer after enquiry was satisfied with the above Statement and handed them over to be dealt with by the BELGIAN authorities for breach of regulations. A Division Bearers paraded to collect wounded. Patients in Hospital 52. Cars in running Order 7. MAJOR FISHER, Q.M. Sergt PARKER W, Sergt PARKER W, Sergt STOKES R.T. and Pte SUNLEY H. proceeded on 5 days leave from 1-5 Inst.	

LIEUT. COLONEL
COMMANDG 2 NORTHUMBRIAN FIELD
AMBULANCE R.A.M.C. (T.F.)
86 Fld A Amb

121/7381

38th Division

86th Field Ambulance

Vol VII

Aug. Sep 1 & Oct 15

WAR DIARY
INTELLIGENCE SUMMARY of 2nd NORTHUMBRIAN FIELD AMBULANCE, ROYAL ARMY MEDICAL CORPS. (T.F.)

Army Form C. 2118

(Erase heading not required.)

Instructions regarding War Diaries and Intelligence Summaries are contained in F.S. Regs., Part II. and the Staff Manual respectively. Title Pages will be prepared in manuscript.

Place	Date	Hour	Summary of Events and Information	Remarks and references to Appendices
LOCRE	1-8-15		The water supply for use of the Unit and Hospital, which is obtained through Brigade arrangements, has for some days been unsatisfactory. An improvement of however noticeable today, owing to the pumps near fort drawing such water having been cleaned and generally overhauled.	J.M.Cameron Lt.Col. O/C 86 Field
"	2-8-15		Lt. INGH. visited the Poelot on which the Unit is at present working, to see if there were any suitable buildings which could be used for an Advanced Dressing Station. The only place which he considered at all suitable was a cellar of a building (RY FARM) which had been shelled, situated at LINDENHOEK. The A.D.M.S. of the 25th Division who inspected the place, did not however think it quite suitable.	S.M.I
"	3-8-15		The O.C. visited Sector, for the purpose of finding suitable place for Advance Dressing station. During the night the enemy, by means of a mine, blew up one of our Trenches. 14 men were traced of. One of the men remained buried for 16½ hours and was eventually brought in. It is interesting to note that this man was without doubt saved, owing to the special knowledge of the mining section of the 1st Monmouth Regiment, as by scratching with their hands, they were able to keep an passage though to the man, until proper implements were available.	J.C

J.M.Cameron
LIEUT. COLONEL
COMMANDG (2 NORTHUMBRIAN) FIELD
AMBULANCE R.A.M.C. (T.F.)

WAR DIARY
OF
~~INTELLIGENCE SUMMARY~~ 86 (2ND NORTHUMBRIAN) FIELD AMBULANCE,
ROYAL ARMY MEDICAL CORPS. (T.F.)
(Erase heading not required.)

Army Form C. 2118

Instructions regarding War Diaries and Intelligence Summaries are contained in F.S. Regs., Part II. and the Staff Manual respectively. Title Pages will be prepared in manuscript.

Place	Date	Hour	Summary of Events and Information	Remarks and references to Appendices
LOCRE	4.8.15.		Three of the Bearer Officers together with a number of the Personnel of the Unit are suffering from Sickness and Diarrhoea probably due to the water supply. The water at present drawn from LOCRE having vegetable matter in it. A sample of the water has been sent to the Sanitary Officer for testing. The sample taken before the water was clarified and one sample after.	J.K.
"	7.8.15		An Officer has today been detailed to visit the 5. K.O.R.L. 2. E. Yorks and a Heavy Battery of Artillery owing to their various medical officers being away on leave. The number of patients admitted to Hospital during past week are as follows Wounded 31. Sick 129. Total 160.	
"	8.8.15.		Sergt Ellison and 12 men were detailed to occupy Dug outs in "ARCADIA" to establish an Advance Post from which Bearers could be called out the evacuation require. They have with them a Sherched Litter and Lakorio for two days. Arrangements are also made to deliver rations at the Barrier daily. As a result of this arrangement it is not now necessary to send out Bearers at night unless the evacuation require it. Also cases can now be evacuated in the day time to the Dugout where Motor Ambulance can meet the cases and bring them on to the Hospital. Arrangements are also made whereby cases are sent down the line to inform us of the number of cases requiring to be evacuated	J.K.

N.K.Innen
LIEUT. COLONEL
COMMANDg (2 NORTHUMBRIAN) FIELD
AMBULANCE R.A.M.C. (T.F.)
3t Field Ambce.

Army Form C. 2118

WAR DIARY
of
INTELLIGENCE SUMMARY
(Erase heading not required.)

Instructions regarding War Diaries and Intelligence Summaries are contained in F. S. Regs., Part II. and the Staff Manual respectively. Title Pages will be prepared in manuscript.

Place	Date.	Hour	Summary of Events and Information	Remarks and references to Appendices
LOCRE	8-8-15		A civilian child having been found dead in a wood in the vicinity of KEMMEL was brought to the hospital by the Provost officer attached to the 5th Lancers. The child had been missing since Wednesday and was found on Saturday afternoon. There were two punctured wounds on the left side of the chest and one on the left side of neck. — After the body, which was in a very decomposed condition, had been viewed it was placed in the mortuary to await a post mortem examination and is awaiting still at AREDIA kept under observation. — One of the men doing duty at KEMMEL was detailed for duty at Headquarters of 6th Welsh to keep up intercommunication between the Headquarters and the Advanced Post.	J.C.
	9-8-15		Lieut A.C.C. LAWRENCE reported the Unit for duty after being away to ENGLAND on sick leave. — Lt Col ROCH D.A.D.M.S. 28th Division and MAJOR ADDERLEY D.A.D.M.S. of one of the New Armies who were on an instructional tour visited and inspected the hospital. Acting on instructions received from D.A.D.M.S. 28th Division, 6 Bell tents were handed over to 6th Batt'n Leicester Regt. 110 Brigade, 37 Division. — Under instructions from A.D.M.S. 28th Division, two motor cycles, to complete establishment of 3 cycles authorised by A.F. G 1098-63 B dated April, were indented for on Armed Depot, Mechanical Transport ABBEVILLE. The D.D.S of T informed to empty vans, as he informed me that as a Field Ambulance (Territorial) attached to a Regular Division, we are regarded as a Regular Field Ambulance not entitled to more than one W.H.C.	

J. R. Amun
LIEUT. COLONEL
COMMAND'G (2 NORTHUMBRIAN) FIELD AMBULANCE R.A.M.C. (T.F.) & Lt Amfse.

Army Form C. 2118

WAR DIARY
or
INTELLIGENCE SUMMARY

5th (2ND NORTHUMBRIAN) FIELD AMBULANCE, ROYAL ARMY MEDICAL CORPS. (T.F.)

(Erase heading not required.)

Instructions regarding War Diaries and Intelligence Summaries are contained in F. S. Regs., Part II. and the Staff Manual respectively. Title Pages will be prepared in manuscript.

Place	Date	Hour	Summary of Events and Information	Remarks and references to Appendices
LOCRE	10.8.15.		Capt MACNEE. R.A.M.C visited Hospital and took samples of blood from a number of patients in Hospital, suffering from suspected typhoid fever at Dunch Street.	M.
"	11.8.15.		Apparatus for heating water for metallic Dermany received today from No 2 Advanced Medical Store. We are still without the apparatus for heating water for Syringe mount, which I asked for by A.D.M.S. during the period the O.C. was on leave.	F.
"	12.8.15		Whilst the Germans were shelling part of our Area, the concussion caused by a shell bursting upset two candles which were on a table on which were some papers in the dugout occupied by one of the Battalions. As a result of this the papers were set alight. Sergt Gleeson of this Unit who happened to be near at the time, went into the room and put out the fire. But for the prompt action of this N.C.O. the place would in all probability have been burned down. Wire received from Brigade Major. 5th Bde Brigade complaining that our men were using Dug out as Advanced Post. O.C. visited Brigade Major during the afternoon who only granted permission for the men to remain there on condition they should vacate the Dug out at a moment's notice.	?b.i.stat.

J.P.Gunson

LIEUT. COLONEL
COMMANDG (2 NORTHUMBRIAN) FIELD
AMBULANCE R.A.M.C. (T.F.)
& Field Ambce.

1875 Wt. W593/826 1,000,000 4/15 J.B.C. & A. A.D.S.S./Forms/C. 2118.

Army Form C. 2118

WAR DIARY
or
INTELLIGENCE SUMMARY

(Erase heading not required.)

86th (2ND NORTHUMBRIAN) FIELD AMBULANCE,
ROYAL ARMY MEDICAL CORPS. (T.F.)

Instructions regarding War Diaries and Intelligence Summaries are contained in F. S. Regs., Part II. and the Staff Manual respectively. Title Pages will be prepared in manuscript.

Place	Date	Hour	Summary of Events and Information	Remarks and references to Appendices
LOCRE	13.8.15		Instructions were given to Sergt Ellison that one man was to be detailed for duty at Brigade Headquarters at KEMMEL for keeping up communication between Headquarters and Advance Post. Two men were also detailed for duty at Aid Post in KEMMEL for the purpose of dressing and sending back down to Ambulance Cars of the Barret.	
"	14.8.15		MAJOR-GENERAL E.S.BULFIN, C.V.O, C.B, G.O.C 28 Division visited and inspected the Hospital today. The number of Patients admitted to Hospital during the week are as follows: Wounded 15 Sick 145. Total 160. -	
"	16.8.15		A concert was given to the Patients in Hospital and the Personnel of the Unit by the 28th Divisional Concert Party "The Dugouts". The party consists of Lt. HORNE A.D.C & G.O.C Division and of Despatch Riders. A most enjoyable evening was spent. There was also a large number of visitors from the various Regiments in the Division.	
"	17.8.15		A Sergt Major of the 1st Welsh Regt who was a Patient in Hospital suggested a method of smashing mosquitos etc on the premises. The suggestion was adopted and found very satisfactory. The nessy was supplied by O.C Sanitary Section, and the frames were made by men of this Unit.	

D. Munro
LIEUT. COLONEL
COMMANDS 86 NORTHUMBRIAN (T.F.)
AMBULANCE R.A.M.C. (T.F.)
86 Fd Amb

Army Form C. 2118

WAR DIARY
OF
INTELLIGENCE SUMMARY 96th (2nd NORTHUMBRIAN) FIELD AMBULANCE,
ROYAL ARMY MEDICAL CORPS, (T.F.)
(Erase heading not required.)

Instructions regarding War Diaries and Intelligence Summaries are contained in F. S. Regs., Part II. and the Staff Manual respectively. Title Pages will be prepared in manuscript.

Place	Date	Hour	Summary of Events and Information	Remarks and references to Appendices
LOCRE	18-8-15		LT D R E ROBERTS was detailed for temporary duty as Medical Officer with the 6th Welsh Regt.	
"	19-8-15		LT A.C.C. LAWRENCE attended the sick of the 2nd Cheshire Regt. as the request of MAJOR MONTGOMERY-SMITH. COL. GEDDES D.D.M.S 2nd Corps accompanied by A.D.M.S. 28th Division visited and inspected the hospital. Complaint received from O.C. 1st Welsh by G.O.C. 84th Brigade re statement made by Major FISHER investigated by A.D.M.S. Here. A letter of explanation sent by Major FISHER.	
"	20-8-15		A complaint was received by O.C. from Sergt Ellison that the men attended for duty at Advance Dri had been ordered up to trenches by a Barrenetti Medical Officer. The matter was reported to A.D.M.S who gave instructions that the men were to abide by the eighteen instructions they had already received. MAJOR FISHER and LT WARDLE were sent sick to Officers Rest Station MONT NOIR.	
"	21.		The number of patients admitted to hospital during the past week are as follows:— Wounded 29. Sick 102. Total 131. JT Munson	

Army Form C. 2118

WAR DIARY
of
INTELLIGENCE SUMMARY
(Erase heading not required.)

86th (2ND NORTHUMBRIAN) FIELD AMBULANCE, ROYAL ARMY MEDICAL CORPS, (T.F.)

Instructions regarding War Diaries and Intelligence Summaries are contained in F.S. Regs., Part II. and the Staff Manual respectively. Title Pages will be prepared in manuscript.

Place	Date	Hour	Summary of Events and Information	Remarks and references to Appendices
LOCRE	23.8.15		Original Regimental Belts, sent by request of Paymaster, to Clearing House Base.	
"	24.8.15		Lt. T.O. INCH was detailed for Temporary Duty with 1st Support Regt. MAJOR D.L. FISHER returned for duty from MONT NOIR. Capt. MACNEE R.A.M.C. again visited the Hospital and took samples of blood from various patients, for examination in French Fort.	
"	25.8.15		A.D.M.S. and Lt. Col R. HENVEY A.A. & Q.M.G. 28 Division visited and inspected Hospital. SURGEON-GENERAL PORTER. D.M.S. 2nd Army and Lt. Col. CHOPPING D.A.D.M.S. 2nd Army visited and inspected Hospital. They were conducted round the Hospital by Capt G.R. ELLIS. Lt. U.H. WARDLE returned for duty from MONT NOIR.	
"	28.8.15		Col GEDDES O.D.M.S. 2nd Corps and the D.A.D.M.S. 28 Division visited the Hospital. The number of Patients admitted during week was wounded 33, Sick 134 Total 167.	
"	29.8.15		As the Hospital of the D.A.D.M.S. O.C visited the Australian Base Hospital WIMEREUX to see an exhibition of splints and unusual drainage	

D.M. Cameron
LIEUT. COLONEL
COMMANDg (2 NORTHUMBRIAN) FIELD AMBULANCE, R.A.M.C. (T.F.)
86 Field Amb.

Army Form C. 2118

WAR DIARY
or
INTELLIGENCE SUMMARY 86

(1/4 (2ND NORTHUMBRIAN) FIELD AMBULANCE,
ROYAL ARMY MEDICAL CORPS, (T.F.))

(Erase heading not required.)

Instructions regarding War Diaries and Intelligence Summaries are contained in F. S. Regs., Part II. and the Staff Manual respectively. Title Pages will be prepared in manuscript.

Place	Date	Hour	Summary of Events and Information	Remarks and references to Appendices
LOCRE.	30.8.15		Lt Col. H. B. FAWCUS. G.M.G. D.A.D.M.S. 2nd Corps visited and inspected the hospital.	
"	31.8.15		O.C. visited A.D.M.S. Office for conference of O.Cs Field Ambulances in the 28 Division with D.A.D.M.S of Division in reference to choice of New Adv. Post in case of change in Infantry division. Number of Patients admitted to Hospital since the 28th: Wounded 4. Sick 41. Total 45.	

J.T.Owen

LIEUT. COLONEL
COMMANDG (2 NORTHUMBRIAN) FIELD
AMBULANCE R.A.M.C. (T.F.)
St Field Amb.

1875 Wt. W593/826 1,000,000 4/15 J.B.C. & A. A.D.S.S./Forms/C. 2118.

WAR DIARY or INTELLIGENCE SUMMARY

Army Form C. 2118

2nd (Northumbrian) Field Ambulance

(Erase heading not required.)

Instructions regarding War Diaries and Intelligence Summaries are contained in F.S. Regs., Part II. and the Staff Manual respectively. Title Pages will be prepared in manuscript.

Place	Date	Hour	Summary of Events and Information	Remarks and references to Appendices
LOCRE	1-9-15		Owing to the inclement weather great difficulty has been experienced in getting rid of the organic manure by incineration & in spite of the fact that we have 3 large Incinerators to burn up the rubbish. The manure from the transport not however now got rid of by leading to fields a distance from the Billets and used as manure	
	6-9-15		On instructions from A.D.M.S. Lt Scott reported for duty (temporary) with 3rd Bde Field Artillery but on doing so was informed that the M.O. who had been ill had recovered. He therefore returned to this unit. He was also informed that A.D.M.S. had been asked to provide temporary M.O. about 4 days prior to his giving instructions	
	7-9-15		A.D.M.S. to be taking for prospective A.D. Pds. A.D.M.S. & D.A.D.M.S. visited and inspected hospital. Lt Searle 3rd Bde A.C. died as a result of injuries received owing to falling off a waggon. Lt Ainroth Wright & A.D.M.S. 28 Division visited hospital	
	8-9-15		Lt Roberts left for 14 days leave of absence	
	10-9-15		O.C., A.D.M.S. & D.A.D.M.S. 28 Division went to Kemmel Hill for purpose of selecting position for Adv. pos. to	
	12-9-15		Col Ferguson A.D.M.S. 28 Division who having been appointed D.D.M.S. 12 Corps visited hospital & said goodbye.	
	14-9-15		Col Tapscho on being appointed A.D.M.S. 28 Division visited hospital	
	15-9-15		Instructions received from A.D.M.S. 28 Division a party of men were detailed under Lt Lyall to go to Wilburghem to prepare Dug outs which had to be used as Adv. Pos.	
	17-9-15		Court of enquiry composed of Col Whale, Major Montgomery Smith & Lt Perrett assembled at hospital to enquire into cause of accident which happened to one of the bear stretchers to Lt Lusc	
	20-9-15		O.C. visited A.D.M.S. office for conference of O.Cs. the Field Ambulances in the Division	

J. R. Cameron
No. 26 Field Ambulance
Lieut Colonel

Army Form C. 2118

WAR DIARY
or
INTELLIGENCE SUMMARY
(Erase heading not required.)

H.Q. (Northumbrian) Field Ambulance

Instructions regarding War Diaries and Intelligence Summaries are contained in F. S. Regs., Part II and the Staff Manual respectively. Title Pages will be prepared in manuscript.

Place	Date	Hour	Summary of Events and Information	Remarks and references to Appendices
BETHUNE	1-10-15		J.C. visited ADMS office at SAILLY LE BOURSE for Conference of O's Field Amb	
"	2.10.15		"	
"	3.10.15		"	
"	4.10.15		"	
"	5.10.15		Lieut Macpherson D.D.M.S. 1st Army visited Hospital & inspected the wards & hospital generally. During stay at BETHUNE 800 sick & wounded were received into hospital	
"	6.10.15	4	ended when received from A Div'l. Unit marched to BUSNETTE.	
"	"	5pm	Arrived at BUSNETTE. Personnel billeted in Barns.	
"	"		ADMS & DADMS 28 Division visited Billets	
"	"		While at this Billet the Unit has to undergo a vigorous training. Physical Drill and long route marches have to be done every day	
"	8.10.15		D.D.M.S. 1st Corps visited Billets	

V. Dawson
Lieut Colonel
OC 86 Field Ambulance

Army Form C. 2118

WAR DIARY
or
INTELLIGENCE SUMMARY
(Erase heading not required.) 86/2 (Northumbrian) Field Ambulance

Place	Date	Hour	Summary of Events and Information	Remarks and references to Appendices
BUSNETTES	10/10/15		O.C. visited MONT BERNONCHON and saw trenches being prepared. O8 arranged with officer in charge party for this unit to execute evacuating wounded. 4 tents sent to divisional unit for instructions from A.D.M.S. to enlighten transport too.	
"	"		Lt. MACLAGAN Medical Officer 9 Royal Fusiliers brought to OC notice an excellent method of introducing drugs hypodermically. This continues has them in the common field ambulance. It consists of a collapsible tube to which is attached a hypodermic needle and a protecting cap, and containing a single dose of morphia &c. They are simple and ready for use, and a great improvement on anything at present in use.	
"	11/10/15		Unit engaged on route march. Dinner served on march.	
"	12/10/15		A proportion of the personnel of the Unit had baths at LOCRE.	
"	13/10/15		Instructions received for Unit to carry 50 stretchers, 200 pairs Red Socks and 200 Red Slippers. Capt Wilson constructed a special stretcher for use in narrow angular trenches. This stretcher was brought to notice of A.D.M.S., D.A.D.M.S. 28 Division and D.D.M.S. 1 Corps.	
"	16/10/15		Instructions received for unit to proceed to BETHUNE.	
"	"	2 pm	Unit paraded in full marching order + proceeded BETHUNE to take over hospital	

V.R. Macron Lieut Colonel
o/c 86 Field Ambulance

Army Form C. 2118

WAR DIARY
or
INTELLIGENCE SUMMARY
(Erase heading not required.)

1/1st Northumbrian Field Ambulance

Instructions regarding War Diaries and Intelligence Summaries are contained in F. S. Regs., Part II. and the Staff Manual respectively. Title Pages will be prepared in manuscript.

Place	Date	Hour	Summary of Events and Information	Remarks and references to Appendices
BETHUNE	16.10.15		ECOLE JULES FERRY. Arriving at 4.30 p.m.	
"	17.10.15		Spent cleaning up billet.	
"	18.10.15		Handed instructions received from April 28 Division Lt ROBERTS and Sergt Bell went to take over Ad Posts from the 7E RUT Division	
"	19.10.15		"C" Section Reserve Sub Division was detailed to occupy advance posts at MARRAIS. Units evacuated Hospital at ECOLE JULES FERRY and took over Hospital at ECOLE LIBRE DE GARÇON. This Billet was in a filthy condition & the unit were employed until late at night cleaning the place.	Maj BETHUNE Combined Stabs Rendered Signed W B 7.1.44
"	20.10.15	3.45 p.m.	Acting orders received and communicated the Ambulance and proceeded to PONT D'AVELETTE near BETHUNE men billeted in 2 Farms officers billeted in cottage horses picketed in Fields adjoining. Our horses were exchanged today 21 Heavy draught being exchanged for 43 Light Draught	

D K Lumm Lieut Col
Op 1st Field Ambulance

1875 Wt. W593/826 1,000,000 4/15 J.B.C. & A. A.D.S.S./Forms/C. 2118.

Army Form C. 2118

WAR DIARY
or
INTELLIGENCE SUMMARY
(Erase heading not required.)

Instructions regarding War Diaries and Intelligence Summaries are contained in F. S. Regs., Part II. and the Staff Manual respectively. Title Pages will be prepared in manuscript.

Place	Date	Hour	Summary of Events and Information	Remarks and references to Appendices
LOCRE	21.10.15		The Canadian Contingent having relieved the Division to which this Field Ambulance is attached, the Hospital at the Convent St Antoine was today handed over to the 6th Canadian Field Ambulance	
	22.10.15	12 noon	Left LOCRE and proceeded by march route to MERRIS. The Unit marched well.	
		3.20 p.m.	Arrived at MERRIS. The Personnel of Unit were until canvas. Horse Ambulances were detailed to follow up the Brigade to pick up any men who might fall out.	
	23.10.15		OC visited A.D.M.S. 55th Brigade. A.D.M.S. & D.A.D.M.S. 28 Division visited & inspected Bush Hospital. A Hospital was opened out at Hellebot House Merris having accommodation for about 40 patients.	
	24.10.15		By order of the A.D.M.S. 28 Division 4 cars were sent to LOCRE today to pick up the men of the Church Market Battery. The men did not turn up. Where reported to Corps.	
	25.10.15		Having received instructions to proceed to MERVILLE the Hospital was evacuated and patients sent to HAZEBROUCK and MONT DESCATS. The Equipment of Unit was loaded up on wagons.	
	26.10.15	7.0 a.m.	Unit paraded in full marching order to proceed to MERVILLE.	
		11.45 "	Arrived MERVILLE.	
		12 noon	Moved off from MERVILLE for Colomé and on arriving there, tents were pitched and dinner served. Orders retired for Unit to proceed to BETHUNE.	
		6.30 p.m.	Arrived BETHUNE and Billeted in 2 Estaminets and some stables att to a Chateau. Horses picketed magmes pusked on Boulevard.	
		12 mdt night	Brigade Major 85 Brigade visited OC and orders for moving tomorrow.	

D.R. Cameron
Lieut Colonel
OC 85 Field Ambulance

WAR DIARY
or
INTELLIGENCE SUMMARY
(Erase heading not required.)

Army Form C. 2118

Instructions regarding War Diaries and Intelligence Summaries are contained in F.S. Regs., Part II. and the Staff Manual respectively. Title Pages will be prepared in manuscript.

Place	Date	Hour	Summary of Events and Information	Remarks and references to Appendices
BETHUNE	27.10.15	10.15 am	Unit paraded full marching order and marched to BAILEY-LE-BOURSE. 4 N.C.Os and 16 men were sent to CAMBRIN to go up to aid post to collect wounded. 2 parties of 1 N.C.O. + 8 men were sent to 59 Field Ambulance to act as bearing party to assist 29 Field Ambulance. The remainder of the Unit spent the night under canvas in a field. Things were not improved by the down pour of rain which lasted practically all night.	
SAILEY-LE-BOURSE	28.10.15		All available Bearers and personnel of Unit Sub-Divisions sent to the H.Q. of 85" Brigade for duty. CAPT WILSON was in charge of the party.	
"	"	6.15 pm	Transport Section and details left BAILEY-LE-BOURSE for BETHUNE via CAMBRIN-BOURNEY Road. While transport was halted on road the Bohund was subject to shell fire from the enemy. The wagons were parked in a field. Officers and personnel billeted in houses near 27 Field Ambulance at ECOLE JULES FERRY.	
"	29.10.15	2.30 pm	The Transport Section + details were ordered to proceed to BETHUNE and relieve the	
BETHUNE	"	4 pm	Arrived BETHUNE. Took over Hospital at 6 pm. 60 patients awaited arrival for dressing.	
"	30.10.15		D.D.M.S. 1st Corps visited Hospital. This Unit is now attached to 1st Corps. 1st Army.	

www.ingramcontent.com/pod-product-compliance
Lightning Source LLC
Chambersburg PA
CBHW081555160426
43191CB00011B/1933